U.S.S. CONSTITUTION

1817

OLD IRONSIDES

OLD IRONSIDES

An Illustrated History of *USS Constitution*

Thomas P. Horgan
Captain, USNR (Ret.)

YANKEE

YANKEE INC.
DUBLIN, NEW HAMPSHIRE

OLD IRONSIDES

Ay, tear her tattered ensign down!
    Long has it waved on high,
And many an eye has danced to see
    That banner in the sky;
Beneath it rung the battle shout,
    And burst the cannon's roar;—
The meteor of the ocean air
    Shall sweep the clouds no more!

Her deck, once red with heroes' blood,
    Where knelt the vanquished foe,
When winds were hurrying o'er the flood,
    And waves were white below,
No more shall feel the victor's tread,
    Or know the conquered knee;—
The harpies of the shore shall pluck
    The eagle of the sea!

Oh, better that her shattered hulk
    Should sink beneath the wave;
Her thunders shook the mighty deep,
    And there should be her grave;
Nail to the mast her holy flag,
    Set every threadbare sail,
And give her to the god of storms,
    The lightning and the gale!

Oliver Wendell Holmes, 1830

Table of Contents

Foreword

Wouldn't you like to have known George Washington, or Abraham Lincoln, or Robert E. Lee, in the flesh? Too bad you can't, but you can do the next best thing. You can see, admire, go on board, and walk the decks "once red with heroes' blood" of *USS Constitution*. Built during Washington's administration, she was the fightin'est frigate in the U. S. Navy during three wars, and has remained a national symbol in subsequent wars. Piously preserved through the devotion of the Navy and the American people, she is on view in all her pristine beauty, with guns mounted, yards crossed, and colors flying.

Think of all the great seamen who have commanded *Constitution* and served in her; the victories that this "Eagle of the Sea" has won, the tens of thousands of miles she has sailed with no other power than the brave winds; the flags she has flown, starting with thirteen stars and now fifty; "and many an eye has danced to see that banner in the sky."

USS Constitution is not only an authentic ship of the old sailing navy; she and her history are symbolic of the Navy, of its guts and gallantry and know-how; the armed service that has always protected us in time of war and has shown the flag around the world on friendly missions in time of peace.

In this book, Captain Thomas P. Horgan, USNR (Ret.) has given us the gist of her colorful history, and I commend it to all Americans and all lovers of ships and sailing everywhere. She is an integral part of our country; an assurance that as long as Americans prize valor and as long as they will maintain a fighting navy, they will be an independent, powerful, and free people.

Samuel E. Morison

Samuel Eliot Morison
Rear Admiral, USNR (Ret.)
Professor of American History, Emeritus,
Harvard University

Introduction

by Theodore Thomte

Old Ironsides has been a source of inspiration to many Americans. Writing of her, President John F. Kennedy said, "My earliest memories of the United States Navy go back to the days when, as a small boy, I used to be taken to (visit) *Constitution* in Charlestown, Massachusetts. The sight of that historic frigate, with its tall spars and black guns, stirred my imagination and made American history come alive for me. I know that a visit to Old Ironsides has done the same for many thousands of young Americans."

Visiting Old Ironsides has "made American history come alive" for millions of citizens of all ages. This illustrated introduction is offered to combine a sketch of *Constitution's* history with the visitor's visual impressions. These first pages only hint at the fullness and richness of the story of *Constitution* which unfolds as you savor Captain Thomas P. Horgan's *Old Ironsides*.

People who have known Old Ironsides through the years have come to feel she has a personality all her own. Many old-time sailors would no more say "the *Constitution*," than they would refer to a man named Jones as "the Jones." To those who have known and loved her, a ship is very much a person. So it is with Old Ironsides — she is simply *Constitution* to most who know her well, and we invite readers of this book to join in that feeling.

A ship is always spoken of as female. Here we tell the story of *Constitution* — the story of *her* battles and *her* history. Most Americans find it natural to think of *Constitution* as a woman — with grace, beauty, independence, strength, self-reliance. vitality — and with thoughts of loyalty and love. *Constitution* was thoughtfully conceived and intelligently developed for the best use of the qualities of excellence that were her heritage. She was not built for the shallows; operating in the deeps, she suffered the scars of battle and endured myriad other hardships. She matured and gained respect and love through the harsh tests of difficult times. She has faithfully served those who have loved her from her youth to her mature years. Now, she rests secure, having developed a fullness and completeness that is one of the deepest compliments that can be paid any woman of either sea or land.

Constitution is a part of each American's heritage.
All of us are something more than the sum
total of all we have been.

The frigate *Constitution* slid into the sea on October 21, 1797 at Hartt's Shipyard on Boston's thriving waterfront. Her story starts three years before her tall masts rose to meet the breeze from the sea, when a group of men sat down to discuss a serious danger to the young United States — pirates.

After the Revolutionary War, America almost completely disbanded her armed forces. The new government commanded not a single man-of-war. In March of 1794 President George Washington sent a message to Congress detailing the outrages against American ships and seamen committed by Algerian pirates. That same month the President signed into law a bill Congress had passed at his request. It included authorization to construct or purchase six frigates for use against the Algerian corsairs. Measures were taken immediately to start construction on six of the best frigates the world would ever know.

Constitution was one of the half dozen ships that were the beginning of the permanent Navy of the United States. Her designer, Joshua Humphreys of Philadelphia, believed that these ". . . vessels should combine such qualities of strength, durability, swiftness of sailing, and force as to render them superior to any frigate belonging to the European powers." With a mere handful of ships the United States Navy could scarcely afford to lose a single one in battle.

The frigate *Constitution* is America's most famous fighting ship.

Ton for ton, gun for gun, *Constitution* was designed to be faster, tougher, and more heavily gunned than any enemy ship of her rating.

When Humphreys submitted his designs and specifications, he pointed out the unusual features. Great length. depth. and beam, and large sail area were to be protected by unusually heavy construction coupled with many powerful guns. She carried more sail area than other 44-gun frigates of the day. These frigates would be able to engage in battle or escape from any enemy as their captains chose. They would be free to run or fight at will.

14

U.S. FRIGATE CONSTITUTION
SPAR DECK

Constitution was designed to outsail any ship she could not outfight.

U.S. FRIGATE CONSTITUTION
GUN DECK

In 1798 France and England were locked in the bitter tangle of the Napoleonic wars that would engage the two nations for years to come. Both France and England continually interfered with American shipping, but France's repeated violations against American neutrality finally forced Congress to break all treaties with America's former Revolutionary ally and the small United States Navy was directed to seek out armed French ships. The Quasi War with France had begun.

Commanded by Captain Samuel Nicholson, *Constitution* first cleared for sea from Boston on the evening of July 22, 1798. She captured the 24-gun privateer *Niger* on her first mission of war, bringing her prize and 70 prisoners into Norfolk. Successful duty in the West Indies followed for *Constitution*.

The war at sea went badly for France, and she signed a peace treaty with America in 1801. *Constitution's* first sea duty had gone well. She returned to her home port of Boston to refit and rest until the needs of the nation called her to sea again.

Pirates from North Africa had roamed the seas in search of plunder for centuries before the United States became a nation. Yankee merchantmen had sailed all over the world, but just after the Revolution, America was without a Navy to protect her commerce.

The Barbary States — Morocco, Algiers, Tunis, and Tripoli — stretched half the length of the Mediterranean, across northern Africa to the Atlantic side of the Straits of Gibraltar. The great maritime nations of Europe, even mighty England, had long bribed the rulers of the desert kingdoms with gold and tribute to keep marauding pirates from interfering with trade. America followed Europe's lead for a time, paying blackmail to pirate leaders.

The ruler of Tripoli, the Bashaw, sent a demand for tribute to the American government. If the money did not arrive within six months, he would declare war on the United States. It was not sent. On May 14, 1801, he ordered the flagstaff of the American consulate cut down.

Even before the Bashaw declared war, a decision had been reached in the new capitol at Washington: a squadron of warships was to be sent to the Mediterranean. For more than two years, the squadron was hampered by not having enough power, but the show of force did much to deter the other Barbary States — Algiers, Morocco, and Tunis.

In 1803, Commodore Edward Preble took command of America's small Mediterranean squadron. His flagship was *Constitution*. She and the frigate *Philadelphia* were supplemented by five handy, shallow-draft vessels.

Constitution carried more than 400 officers and men, from some experienced veterans of the Revolutionary War to young midshipmen living in quarters on the third deck. It was to be a long deployment. Unlike most sea voyages of the time, however, plenty of fresh meat, fruits, and vegetables were available from the lush Mediterranean farmlands.

The second most powerful ship in the American squadron, the 36-gun frigate *Philadelphia*, fell into pirate hands after she ran aground on some uncharted rocks. Captain William Bainbridge, having no means of defending his ship, ordered *Philadelphia's* pumps choked, her magazines drowned, and holes cut in the hull. He hauled down his colors as the Tripolitan pirate gunboats closed in, capturing all hands. The pirates succeeded in refloating *Philadelphia* and brought her into Tripoli.

In a letter smuggled to Commodore Preble from prison, Captain Bainbridge suggested that *Philadelphia* be destroyed. Stephen Decatur was put in command of a small, captured Tripolitan ketch which Preble aptly renamed *Intrepid* and had her loaded with combustibles, including casks of precious gunpowder from *Constitution's* magazines.

Disguised as a merchant ship out of Malta, *Intrepid* quietly slipped into the pirate stronghold on the night of February 16, 1804. Decatur and his men boarded *Philadelphia* and after a short battle overpowered all the pirates aboard. He immediately set fire to her storerooms and gunrooms.

One of *Constitution's* midshipmen told the story this way when he wrote home: "... Tripolitans on board her were dreadfully alarmed when they found who we were. Poor fellows! About 20 of them were cut to pieces & the rest jumped overboard ... it was a miracle that our little vessel escaped the flames lying within two feet of them & to leeward."

The raid was a success. *Intrepid* swept from port without the loss of a single life. With the burning of *Philadelphia*, America's major loss of the war was not allowed to become the pirate's gain.

England's Lord Nelson called
the burning of *Philadelphia*
" . . . the most bold and daring
act of the age."

Commodore Preble's blockade of Tripoli had prevented supplies from reaching the port by sea and his tactics were beginning to take effect, with the entire country feeling the pinch. The time had come for the next step in Preble's plan: the bombardment of Tripoli.

He had assembled every ship in the squadron. In all, he commanded 1,060 men. Against them was all of the power of the Bashaw: 115 guns in permanent battery positions, most of them heavy, and 19 gunboats, many able to fire as much metal as a frigate. The harbor defenses were manned by 25,000 Arabs and Turks.

With covering fire from the larger ships in the squadron, the American gunboats closed with the enemy.

In hand-to-hand combat, at which the pirates were supposed to be the best in the world, the Americans triumphed, even though their gunboats were badly outnumbered, suffering only 14 casualties.

Preble's continuing bombardment of Tripoli, and his general conduct of the campaign, did much to win America's victory over the Barbary pirates. On the whole, Preble's command had been highly successful; casualties had been light and during that time not a single man had lost his life on the decks of *Constitution*. One of Preble's greatest contributions was his influence over the junior officers in the squadron. All the captains and lieutenants were under thirty years of age, and it came to be a mark of pride to have served with him. They were "Preble's boys" and proud of it.

Captain John Rodgers was in command of the Mediterranean squadron when the peace treaty with Tripoli was finally signed in the captain's cabin aboard *Constitution* on June 3, 1805.

James Fenimore Cooper, in his *History of the Navy*, wrote, "Perhaps no service, either in the way of ships or officers, ever had so large a proportion of what was excellent in it, and so small a proportion of that which was defective, as the Navy of the United States, the day peace was signed with Tripoli."

The United States Navy developed into an effective fighting force during the Barbary Wars. Morale was high, discipline stern but just, and gunnery and seamanship were of the highest order.

The year 1812 was a year of war. England was bitterly fighting Napoleon's forces and the demands of the long struggle had greatly expanded her forces at sea; thus she sought every available seaman. War with America was the result of English officers boarding American merchant ships and impressing sailors to serve the King of England. Although few Americans were in sympathy with Napoleon, now, in 1812, England's high-handed action against crewmen aboard American ships brought on another war with Great Britain.

England's war against France continued, but by the time war with America came, the demands of the Royal Navy were fewer than they had been in earlier years. British action had reduced the effectiveness of the French fleet, and Spain was no longer hostile to England.

Counting every seaworthy ship of 12 guns or more in the American Navy in 1812, the total was 17, none larger than a frigate. Indeed, there were only eight effective frigates.

Ships of the Royal Navy outnumbered the Americans by about 40 to 1.

In addition to vastly outnumbering the Americans, the Royal Navy had another major advantage — its reputation was built on more than a thousand victories. Throughout the world men believed that an English man-of-war was invincible.

Constitution was vitally needed by the Americans, but she was almost lost on her first cruise of 1812. Captain Isaac Hull sailed *Constitution* from Annapolis on July 12, 1812 and headed north to join an American squadron out of New York. He was off the New Jersey coast, early in the afternoon of July 17, when he saw four sails in the distance.

The affairs of men are frequently confused, and in war they usually become worse. From a distance, British and American ships looked similar, and Hull believed he was joining the American squadron. By dawn, as the mists of morning burned off, the identity of the squadron became clear. *Constitution* had two frigates on her lee quarter, and, astern, a 64-gun ship-of-the-line, accompanied by two more frigates. All these ships were flying the English colors.

There was no wind. Hull acted quickly, and hoisted out his boats, sending them ahead to tow the frigate. He knew the British would follow this tactic, so at the same time he pulled one 18-pounder off the forecastle and another off the spar deck, and set them up as stern chasers. Below decks, he had two 24-pounders run out from the windows of his cabin. Now, if the enemy boats came within range, he could fire at them even though they were astern.

Later, using *Constitution's* boats, Hull set anchors out ahead of the ship and *Constitution's* crew literally hauled the frigate through the water to outdistance her enemies.

During the exciting three-day chase, Isaac Hull saved *Constitution* by outsailing and outwitting some of the best in seamanship and command that England had to offer. Her later victories over ships of the Royal Navy forced England, weary of war from her long battles with Napoleon, to sign a reasonable peace with the Americans. Considering the impact *Constitution's* victories had in the United States and in England, it is interesting to speculate on what the loss of this single ship might have meant to the course of history.

Guerriere was considered one of the best frigates in the Royal Navy when she met Constitution on August 19, 1812.

Guerriere fired first. Constitution closed, holding her fire. Captain Isaac Hull was going to fight on his own terms, close aboard. He brought Constitution's bow in line with Guerriere's stern and gave the order for the first division of guns at the bow: "Fire!" He had laid Constitution alongside at a range of less than half a pistol shot. As she drew abeam, Hull gave Guerriere the rest of his broadside, all guns double-shotted with round and grape inflicting tremendous damage.

Constitution had also stationed sharpshooters in her rigging, firing from her tops, and taking a heavy toll on Guerriere. The two ships were tossing wildly. Hull set canvas to pull away. As Constitution moved ahead, the enemy's foremast fell, carrying with it the mainmast.

All that was left
of the proud frigate *Guerriere*
was a wreck, wallowing
helpless in the sea.

The Royal Navy
had been called unbeatable.
It was no longer true.

Although all men-of-war of the period were similarly constructed, *Constitution* was much more heavily built, using the best materials available. The ship's "knees" were made of live oak and their shape was cut from the natural growth of the tree. The knees were sawed from the base of the tree, with part of the trunk forming one leg and one of the tree's main roots forming the other leg (see opposite page).

The inside planking, as shown here in photo, is called "ceiling." The main frames of the ship are between the ceiling and the outer planking. These details were photographed in the first aid station, forward on the gun deck.

Guerriere had suffered 15 men killed and 63 wounded. *Constitution* suffered only seven killed and seven wounded. Captain James Dacres states he had received 30 shots beneath the waterline, while *Constitution* had suffered virtually no damage to her hull. The Yankee gunners were trained to fire low, and *Guerriere* had seen the result. Expert naval command and gunnery had won the day over the British frigate. Before this victory, the war had not gone well for the Americans. Old Ironsides had earned her place in the hearts and in the history books of the young nation.

Isaac Hull brought *Constitution* into Boston on August 30, 1812 with a shipload of prisoners and the story of America's first decisive naval victory of the war, as the nation went wild with joy.

Making every allowance for a slight advantage *Constitution* had in size, informed men on both sides of the Atlantic, and, indeed, those who were not so well informed, saw future American victories foretold in this single action. To quote Henry Adams: "A small affair it might appear among the world's battles, it took but half an hour, but in that one-half hour the United States rose to the rank of a first-class power."

At the height of the battle, *Constitution* earned her new name as a shot from *Guerriere* rebounded harmlessly off her strongly-constructed hull. Since that August day in 1812 she's been Old Ironsides.

William Bainbridge was in command of *Constitution* when she found the British frigate *HMS Java* off the coast of Brazil on December 29, 1812. At a distance of less than a mile, *Constitution* fired full broadside at 2 p.m. *Java* hoisted the King's colors and returned the fire. Closing to within pistol shot, both ships' long guns and carronades fired round and grape.

Constitution's wheel was shot away and she was difficult to handle, but *Java* was more badly hurt. At 2:50 p.m. she ran afoul of *Constitution's* mizzen rigging. *Java's* bowsprit was next shot away and soon her foremast went over the side.

Bainbridge's journal describes the enemy captain's seamanship and the rest of the action: "At fifteen minutes past three, shot away his main top mast just above the cap. At forty minutes past three, shot away the gaff and spanker boom. At fifty-five minutes past three, shot away his mizzenmast nearly by the board."

Java's gallant commander, Captain Henry Lambert, was fatally wounded in the fight. Bainbridge himself had been hit by a musket ball in the hip early in the fighting. A few minutes later, when *Constitution's* wheel was carried away by a shot, a small copper bolt was driven into the captain's thigh. Despite his wound, he stayed on deck directing the fighting throughout the battle, not going below until well into evening.

As they had done with *Guerriere*, her guns had reduced *Java* to an unmanageable wreck, with every spar shot away and three stumps instead of masts. *Constitution* came " . . . out of the battle as she had gone in, with royal-yards across, and every spar, from the highest to the lowest, in its place," although there was considerable damage to the rigging.

From the point of view of American morale, the victory was of great importance. The whole world recognized that the difference between the power of the two ships was slight, but the difference in results was tremendous.

It was the hardest-fought frigate battle of the war.   The once invincible
Royal Navy took steps to see it would not happen again: they ordered
their frigates never to engage 44-gun American frigates in single action.

In mid-December, 1814, Old Ironsides sailed on her fifth cruise of the War of 1812 — the last war cruise of her glorious career, which would see her win the final great frigate victory of the War of 1812.

The tough, seasoned seamen who manned *Constitution's* main battery, her 24-pounders on the gun deck, were proud of their weapons, which could hurl their solid iron shot about one mile. Unlike the British, who were often stingy in providing gunpowder for practice drills, *Constitution's* gunners were well exercised in their craft.

Sailing off the Madeira Islands on February 20, 1815, *Constitution* was about four miles from the frigate *Cyane* mounting 34 guns and the sloop *Levant*, carrying 20 guns. She opened up at 300 yards and both ships returned the fire.

The frigate *Cyane* was trying to cross *Constitution's* stern in order to rake her. *Constitution's* captain, Captain Charles Stewart, then executed one of the most unusual maneuvers ever seen in the days of fighting sail; he fired a broadside into *Levant*, and, with the smoke covering his action, backed *Constitution* astern, preventing *Cyane* from crossing his own stern and put himself in a position to open fire again.

James Fenimore Cooper called Stewart's action ". . . among the most brilliant maneuvering in naval annals." While not unheard of, the backing of a full-rigged sailing ship was a tricky thing at best. Executed during the heat of battle, it aroused universal admiration.

The victory over *Cyane* and *Levant* was *Constitution's* last battle.

32

The proud frigate *Constitution* has served the United States longer than any warship in history. She continues to serve the Navy and the nation she helped defend — the world's oldest commissioned warship afloat.

The American Navy had gone into the War of 1812 outnumbered by the Royal Navy about 40 to 1, but it won a worldwide reputation. The war ashore had not gone well for the Americans, and naval victories, such as those achieved by *Constitution*, gave heart to the American people. The brilliant victories of the frigate *Constitution* did much to build that reputation and the traditions of the United States Navy.

OLD IRONSIDES

Part I

A Pictorial History

A New Nation

No warship that ever sailed the seas better served her country than "Old Ironsides," *USS Constitution.*

She brought dignity to an infant nation and won the respect and admiration of great world powers—although she often had only grudging support from the country she defended.

She had something more important: the unstinting devotion of a small company of brave men, spirited volunteers, whose seamanship and gunnery never failed to defeat her foes. Service with *Constitution* produced many of the nation's outstanding naval leaders.

The frigate herself was planned and constructed for speed which would enable her to escape any opponent she could not defeat. Her record proves the soundness of this concept, and *Constitution* remains a symbol of the nation's sea power to this day.

After the Revolutionary War, the new United States disbanded her small fleet, wanting only to pursue peaceful commerce on the seas. But the seas were far from peaceful and the nation was powerless to protect her far-ranging merchant vessels. In the Mediterranean, fierce Barbary pirates preyed on merchant ships. American ships also were subject to outrages by both England and France. Great Britain and France were locked in a long and bitter struggle which raged over Europe and the seas. Both countries ignored American rights as a neutral and harassed Yankee shipping with crippling effect. Many American merchants, more concerned with their expanding foreign trade than with their country's honor, wished to avoid war at any cost and felt the way to do so was to purchase immunity and remain unarmed.

In 1785 the United States had not a single armed vessel and only a small sea force when the North African pirates gave America's merchant marine their undivided attention. European nations had made treaties with the pirates—which made sitting ducks of American shipping, the only prey left to the corsairs. European

THE AVENGING EAGLE—*This carved representation of the American eagle is one of four decorating the gangways of Old Ironsides. They well represent the fierce determination of the infant U. S. Navy which made freedom of the seas a national policy. Old Ironsides remains today a symbol of the nation's sea power—the world's oldest warship in commission afloat.*

nations had reason to be pleased with this harassment of a flourishing rival. The ruler of Algiers, the Dey, frankly summed up his situation:

"If I were to make peace with everybody, what should I do with my corsairs? They would take off my head for the want of other prizes, not being able to live on their miserable allowance."

The Algerians captured eleven American merchant vessels within a period of a few weeks in 1793 and imprisoned 106 mariners. There had been ample prior provocation for Congress to act, and it finally did so, apparently stirred by a letter from a captive captain and an accompanying petition signed by thirteen American shipmasters. Captain Richard O'Brien asked for immediate steps to protect our merchant fleet and warned Congress that if this were not done the corsairs would control the Atlantic Ocean and be tempted to raid the coastal waters of the United States. The thirteen captains, in pleading for the prisoners, some of whom had endured eight years of hard labor, wrote:

"Your petitioners pray you will take their unfortunate situation into consideration, and adopt such measures as will restore the American captives to their country, their friends, families and connections; and your petitioners will ever pray and be thankful."

Even though Congress could no longer tolerate international banditry and appropriated funds for six frigates, including *Constitution*, it had stipulated that construction would be halted if immunity for our merchant ships could be purchased through treaty. Such a treaty was obtained from Algiers in 1795 just as *Constitution* and some of the other frigates were nearing completion, and construction was suspended. Terms of the treaty included payment to the Dey of approximately a million dollars in cash, plus the gift of a new frigate and $21,600 in naval stores annually during the life of the treaty. The new frigate named *Crescent* was built at Portsmouth, New Hampshire, at a cost of $100,000. Aboard when she sailed for delivery to the Dey of Algiers was Captain O'Brien, returning as Consul General to all the Barbary States, where

he had been imprisoned for ten years.

The Christian nations of Europe had bowed to extortion by the North African Moors for three centuries. Together, the maritime nations, particularly England, France, and Holland, easily could have ended plundering operations of the Barbary pirates, but in their trade rivalry they felt it more advantageous to keep the robbers in business as a check on competitors.

The Barbary pirates were not alone in refusing to show respect to our young nation. England and France continued their humiliating and hostile acts against the United States, and President George Washington was not happy with a submissive policy. In 1796 he advised Congress:

"It is our experience that the most sincere neutrality is not sufficient guard against the depredations of nations at war. To secure respect to a neutral flag requires a naval force organized and ready to protect it from insult or aggression."

England had long used brutal press gangs to drag her own people from their homes and families to man her fleet. So it was only a short step when they extended this system to the impressment of American merchant seamen, forcing them to serve on British ships. Usually this was done on the pretext they were British subjects.

British and, particularly, French aggression continued, and in July 1797, Congress authorized funds to resume construction of six frigates. *Constitution* was one of the six.

BIRD OF PREY—*This rakish craft was typical of those used by the Barbary pirates in plundering merchant ships. The raiders were fast and were handled skillfully under sail by their fierce crews. They were an elusive foe, for their slight draft often let them escape in waters too shallow for pursuit. Seagoing racketeers, the pirates specialized in robbery, slavery, and the gathering of "protection money."*

Joshua Humphreys' correspondence with Robert Morris, Minister of Finance, may well have won him the assignment to design the six frigates authorized by Congress. Some of his ideas were so sound that they have influenced our naval construction through modern times.

"Sir,-From the present appearance of affairs I believe it is time this country was possessed of a navy; but as that is yet to be raised, I have ventured a few remarks on the subject.

"Ships that compose the European navys are generally distinguished by their rates; but as the situation and depth of water of our coasts and harbors are different in some degrees from those in Europe, and as our navy for a considerable time will be inferior in numbers, we are to consider what size ships will be most formidable, and be an overmatch for those of an enemy; such frigates as in blowing weather would be an overmatch for double-deck ships, and in light winds to evade coming to action; or double-deck ships that would be an overmatch for common double-deck ships, and in blowing weather superior to ships of three decks, or in calm weather or light winds to outsail them. Ships built on these principles will render those of an enemy in a degree useless, or require a greater number before they dare attack our ships. . . . As such ships will cost a large sum of money, they should be built of the best materials that could possibly be procured. . . .

"The greatest care should be taken in the construction of such ships. . .for if we should be obliged to take a part in the present European war, or at a future day we should be dragged into a war with any powers of the Old Continent, especially Great Britain, they having such a number of ships of that size. . .it would be an equal chance by equal combat that we lose our ships. . . . Several questions will arise, whether one large or two small frigates contribute most to the protection of our trade, or which will cost the least sum of money, or whether two small ones are as able to engage a double-deck ship as one large one. For my part I am decidedly of opinion the large ones will answer best."

"Joshua Humphreys"

> W O. July 7th 1797
>
> Sir,
>
> It being necessary to fix on a Name for the Frigate intended for the Dey of Algiers before she sails from Portsmouth: I have therefore concluded to call her the *Crescent*, which Name you will be pleased to have inserted in her papers and other documents —
>
> I have just receiv'd your favor of the 29th Ulto and I congratulate you and Mr Hackett on the safe launching of the Frigate into her proper element.

A BITTER TASK—*The shipwrights of Portsmouth, New Hampshire, who built a fine frigate for the Dey of Algiers in 1797 had little reason to enjoy their labor. The new warship had been exacted under terms of a treaty which sought to purchase immunity for American merchantmen from Algerian corsairs. The frigate, called* Crescent, *after the emblem much used by the Moors, was laden with other tribute and delivered the next year. Apparently, no one recognized in the transaction the arming of a bandit. The Secretary of War was forced to handle the humiliating affair with the best possible grace — as seen in the accompanying letter to the builders. Shipbuilding was handled by the War Office until establishment of the Navy Department in 1798.*

AN EAGLE IN ARMOR— *The American eagle is the national emblem. This fine example of the woodcarver's art graces Old Ironsides' stern. The fearless, feathered warrior reflects the country's early determination to remain free. It was widely used for decoration in sailing-ship days by merchant ships as well as by the Navy. Surviving examples of the almost-lost art have become museum treasures.*

A New Frigate

Constitution was built at Edmund Hartt's shipyard, across Boston Harbor from her permanent berth at the Naval Shipyard. The Coast Guard later established its Boston base at the site. Nearby were Paul Revere's home and the Old North Church.

Although records credit Joshua Humphreys with the basic design of the frigates, he had valuable assistance from others; in particular, Josiah Fox, who was also a skilled naval architect. The two men had something else in common. Both were known as Quakers and their part in producing ships of war disturbed members of the Society of Friends.

When construction of *Constitution* and five other frigates was authorized on March 27, 1794, most of the necessary timber still stood in the forest. Joshua Humphreys specified that only the best be used, and men were sent to scout the forests to find it. Tall pines were felled at Unity, Maine, dragged and rolled to the sea, and towed to Boston for *Constitution's* masts. Large quantities of white oak were obtained in the New England area. But it was necessary to search more widely for "live" oak — so called because its great strength and durability made it the best of all timber for building wooden ships. After scouts located a good supply on a group of islands in Georgia, the government bought three of the islands for $16,000, approximately the value of the live oak needed for the six frigates. Large quantities of yellow pine were brought from Georgia and South Carolina.

Paul Revere, a man of many talents, furnished much of *Constitution's* copper and composition hardware, using his own formulas. Included were bolts, rods and other fastenings, and copper sheathing for her bottom. He had promised the materials "as cheap as any one," and was paid $3,820.33. Anchors were made at Hanover, Massachusetts.

Construction of *Constitution* could proceed only at the pace at which materials arrived. In those days a shipyard little resembled the highly mechanized establishments we see now. All that was required was a piece of shore property suitable for building and launching ways. A hull was fabricated to a great extent by hand labor,

A GALA AFFAIR—*Constitution's launching in 1797 was a festive event which attracted a throng of officials and citizens. In his announcement to the public, the builder spoke of his "...conducting into the ocean, a powerful agent of national justice, which hope dictates may become the just pride and ornament of the American name." This faith in* Constitution *soon was justified. The launching site was directly across the harbor from the present Boston Navy Yard, where* Constitution *has been berthed during most of the years she has not been at sea.*

THE BOS'N PIPES "SET THE WATCH"—*A boatswain's pipe was used to transmit orders to the crew. This ancient instrument, which sounds somewhat like a shrill marsh bird, is still in use in the modern Navy, although its piercing notes usually are relayed electronically. The man shown here wears a uniform patterned after that of sailing-ship days.*

DOWN THE WAYS—*Fears were expressed that* Constitution's *entry into the harbor might cause a minor tidal wave. The public was cautioned to guard against being swept from nearby wharves, but this warning was unnecessary. Note that the artist has pictured the Old North Church between the fore- and mainmasts. From its steeple, Paul Revere received the lantern signal which sent him on his famous ride to alarm the citizenry of the approach of the British in the War of Independence. Revere supplied much of* Constitution's *hardware, including the copper which covers her hull up to the waterline.*

and skilled adzmen made a major contribution. An adz resembles a curved axhead fitted at right angles to the handle. Ship carpenters used them with the care of a sculptor. There were almost no straight lines—curves were almost the rule in building a wooden hull. Few pieces of timber could be cut to the same measure. Shipbuilding had little in common with house carpentry.

In some sections, *Constitution's* hull was protected by more than twenty inches of frames and planking, the heaviest being near the waterline. In general, she was built as strongly as the major war vessels of the time—the line-of-battle ships. Thousands of wooden treenails were used in place of metal spikes to fasten timbers together. Pronounced "trunnels," they usually were made of locust and were immovable after they were swelled by dampness.

Constitution's designed dimensions gave her a length over all of 204 feet and 175 feet on the load waterline; a beam of 43 feet, 6 inches; and her best sailing draft was 21 feet forward and 23 feet aft. Her tonnage under old measurement rules ranged from 1,335 to 1,576 tons. Many years later, the Navy listed her displacement at 2,200 tons, about the same as some World War II destroyers.

Constitution was provided a suit of thirty-six sails, almost all square and made of flax. They had an area of 42,720 square feet, approximately an acre. The largest unit was the 3,400-square-foot main topsail. Well over two miles of hemp cordage were required for running rigging to manage the sails. This did not include standing rigging used to support the masts nor cordage used other places on the ship.

The complexities of this "power plant" give some idea of the importance of the sailing master, whose responsibility was to handle the ship even during the fury of battle. Records indicate *Constitution's* top speed was thirteen and a half knots. Many steam vessels never moved so fast.

Construction of *Constitution* was suspended after the signing of a treaty with Algiers, and it was not until July 1797 that Congress appropriated funds to complete *Constitution*. She was launched October 21, 1797, under circumstances likely to make sailors, always superstitious folk, fear she would be a jinx ship. The launching had been attempted a month earlier, but she stuck on the ways. Force was applied, but she moved only about twenty-five feet before stopping dead as the ways settled. A huge crowd of spectators, which included many notables, went home disappointed. Two days later another thirty feet were gained. After the inclination of the ways was steepened, the launch was completed on October 21 on the next favorable tide.

The other five frigates were completed and launched. They were the 44-gun frigates *President* at New York, *United States* at Philadelphia, *Chesapeake* at Norfolk, and 36-gun *Constellation* at Baltimore and *Congress* at Portsmouth. During construction, *Chesapeake* was changed to a 36-gun rating, leaving the ships evenly divided between 44- and 36-gun frigates.

U.S.S. CONSTITUTION

1817

Quasi War

Our Quasi War with France gave *Constitution* her first active duty in 1798. There was little enthusiasm for conflict with a nation which only two decades earlier had been a valued ally in our War of Independence. However, France forced hostilities by persistent raids on our merchant ships, violations of neutrality, and refusal to deal with our diplomats. Congress finally voided all treaties and directed our naval forces to seek out armed French vessels.

Constitution departed Boston on July 22, 1798, less than a year off the launching ways, and was soon bound for the West Indies. She was unsuited to her task, since most of the French vessels in the area were small, swift privateers which could easily elude a heavy frigate in the shallow, dangerous waters of the Indies. The operations served *Constitution* as little more than a training cruise. The cruise did, however, furnish a preview of her sailing qualities and the skill and daring of a young officer, Lieutenant Isaac Hull, who some years later became one of her most famous commanders.

Constitution, commanded by Commodore Silas Talbot, who had recently relieved her first commander, Samuel Nicholson, was patroling off San Domingo when she encountered the British frigate *Santa Margaretta*. Diplomatically, the two nations were on friendly terms. The British commander, a Captain Parker, was an old acquaintance of Talbot's. The Commodore invited him aboard *Constitution*.

The British were contemptuous of the new American frigates, but the visiting captain professed admiration for *Constitution*. This could have been little more than courtesy because Captain Parker promptly added an opinion that his command could outsail the American ship. Talbot accepted the challenge and a race was arranged for a few weeks later. The stake was a cask of Madeira wine on the challenger's side against its value in cash.

Before the race, the British frigate was tuned up and her bottom cleaned and she reported for the sailing duel as trim as a racing yacht.

A CHAMPION CUTS HER TEETH—*After her launching,* Constitution *was outfitted for sea under the direction of her commander, Captain Samuel Nicholson. She first sailed in 1798. Her builders' predicted speed soon was tested and the powerful new frigate was not found wanting. On one of her early cruises she met a British frigate off the West Indies whose skipper was an acquaintance of Commodore Silas Talbot, who had succeeded Nicholson to the command of* Constitution. *This was during a period of uneasy peace with England. The Britisher came aboard as a visitor and after inspecting* Constitution *proposed a test of speed. England was given a preview of what she was to later encounter in the War of 1812; the challenger was far astern after a dawn-to-dusk sailing duel.*

A DARING RAID—Constitution *was seeking French privateers in May 1800 when Isaac Hull first displayed the skill and courage which later brought him fame. Commodore Talbot assigned Hull, his first lieutenant, and a party of bluejackets and marines to the sloop* Sally *and sent them to cut out the French privateer* Sandwich. *The French ship had taken refuge in the Spanish harbor of Port Platte, San Domingo. The marines spiked harbor guns as sailors from* Sally *boarded and quickly subdued* Sandwich's *crew. Above, marines are shown landing to spike the guns of the fort while* Sally *draws alongside* Sandwich. *At right, Hull's men take the French privateer. Those who took part in the raid were praised, but the seizure in a neutral port was ruled illegal and the prize returned.*

Isaac Hull was made responsible for handling *Constitution*. The starting gun was at dawn; the finish at sunset. The course was directly to windward, the direction from which the wind was blowing. The two frigates beat to windward all day, and on square-rigged vessels this meant a tremendous amount of sail handling. Hull lured his opponent into frequent short tacks instead of sailing long ones, confident *Constitution's* crew would be livelier than the men of *Santa Margaretta*. His reputation for excellence of ship handling, which has never dimmed, was established during this race.

At sunset the British frigate was far astern. When the victor joined the vanquished after dark, Captain Parker was waiting in his gig with the cask of Madeira.

On May 10, 1800, there was another exploit which threw the spotlight on Isaac Hull. Commodore Talbot had discovered a French privateer in the neutral Spanish harbor of Port Platte, San Domingo, West Indies. The incident is best described in Talbot's report to the Secretary of the Navy.

"I have now to acquaint you, Sir, that I have for some time been meditating an enterprise against a French armed ship lying at Port Platte, protected by her own guns and a fort of three heavy cannon. It was my first intention to have gone in with the *Constitution,* and to have silenced the fort and ship, which has all her guns on one side, to cooperate with the fort in defending against any hostile force; but after the best information I could gain, I found it to be somewhat dangerous to approach the entrance of the harbor, with a ship of the draft of water of the *Constitution.*

"Having detained the sloop *Sally. . .*I conceived that this sloop would be a suitable vessel for a disguise. I, therefore, manned her at sea from the *Constitution,* with about ninety brave seamen and marines, the latter to be commanded by Captain Carmick and Lieutenant Amory, when on shore; but the entire command I gave to Mr. Isaac Hull, my first lieutenant, who entered the harbor of Port Platte yesterday in open day, with his men in the hold of the sloop, except five or six to work her in. They ran alongside of the ship, and boarded her sword in hand, without the loss of a man, killed or wounded. At the moment the ship was boarded, agreeably to my plan, Captain Carmick and Lieutenant Amory landed with the marines, up to their necks in water, and spiked all the cannon in the fort, before the commanding officer had time to recollect and prepare himself for defense.

"Perhaps no enterprise of the same moment was ever better executed; and I feel myself under great obligations to Lieutenant Hull, Captain Carmick and Lieutenant Amory, for their avidity in undertaking the scheme I had planned, and for the handsome manner and great address with which they performed this daring venture.

"The ship, I understand, mounts four sixes and two nines; she was formerly the British packet *Sandwich,* and from the boasting publications. . .and the declaration of the officers, she is one of the fastest sailors that swims. She ran three or four years (if I forget not), as a privateer out of France, and with greater success than any other that ever sailed out of their ports. She is a beautiful copper bottomed ship; her cargo consists principally of sugar and coffee."

The capture, however, put no sugar in the coffee of *Constitution's* crew. Our government acknowledged that the seizure in a neutral port was illegal and *Sandwich* was returned, together with damages met, in part at least, by prize money due *Constitution's* crew from other captures.

This did not prevent the Secretary of the Navy from complimenting Commodore Talbot for "protecting with effect a great proportion of our commerce, in laying the foundation of a permanent trade with San Domingo, and in causing the American character to be respected."

A treaty ended hostilities with France in March 1801, and Congress put the Navy on peacetime status although outrages by the Barbary pirates continued. *Constitution* was retired and spent two decommissioned years at the Boston Navy Yard. Then she embarked on her most glorious years by sailing against the corsairs.

INTO THE PIRATES' LAIR—*The worst reverse in the war with Tripoli took place when the corsairs captured* Philadelphia, *for with her went a major part of Commodore Edward Preble's firepower. The loss of the 36-gun frigate was doubly critical because it gave the Tripolitans their most powerful warship. Stephen Decatur volunteered for an extremely perilous mission. On the night of February 16, 1804, he and a company of volunteers glided into the* heavily fortified harbor of Tripoli in a captured ketch, aptly renamed Intrepid. *Decatur's men swarmed aboard* Philadelphia, *routed her pirate crew and set the frigate blazing from stem to stern. They were away within twenty minutes and, as guns of shore batteries and anchored corsairs roared,* Intrepid *escaped without the loss of a man. England's most famous sea lord, Horatio Nelson, called it ". . .the most bold and daring act of the age."*

Barbary Pirates

In 1803, Commodore Edward Preble was assigned to lead an expedition against the Barbary States. This pirate league—Morocco, Algiers, Tunis, and Tripoli—controlled most of the North African coast and had preyed upon the trade of the Christian nations of Europe for three hundred years.

The United States already had some ships in the Mediterranean when Preble arrived with *Constitution*. By November of 1803, the Commodore commanded a well-led force which included *Philadelphia*, a 36-gun frigate (commanded by William Bainbridge); *Argus*, 16 guns (Isaac Hull); *Siren*, 16 guns (Charles Stewart); *Vixen*, 14 guns (John Smith); *Nautilus*, 12 guns (Richard Somers); and *Enterprise*, 12 guns (Stephen Decatur).

Preble summoned the commanding officers to a conference in his cabin after the squadron assembled off the African coast and was disappointed to find none was even thirty years old. Preble was forty-two. Later, when chided for referring to the officers as "boys," Preble quickly amended: "Yes, but they are good boys." This was prophetic, because four—Hull, Bainbridge, Stewart, and Decatur—were among *Constitution's* later commanders.

Preble was one of the ablest mariners of his time. He had left his home on a Maine farm at sixteen to serve at sea in the War of Independence and briefly was a prisoner of the British. After the war he saw much of the world during fifteen years in the merchant marine. He was commissioned as a Navy lieutenant in 1798 and promoted to captain the next year.

At the outset, Preble's severe insistence on proficiency made him unpopular with his command, but under him not a single court-martial was held on *Constitution* and his ability to inspire and train his subordinates produced many of the Navy's most renowned heroes.

Few naval commanders ever operated in a more perilous area. Headquarters for the pirates were at Algiers, Tunis, and Tripoli, along some six hundred miles of the North African Mediterranean shore. This meant a northeasterly wind could trap sailing ships by stranding them along the pirate controlled coast. If driven ashore, a ship's crew could hope for nothing better than cruel enslavement.

Here is an entry from *Constitution's* log: "The weather to the northward has every appearance of a strong breeze from that quarter. A heavy gale from the N.E. or the N.N.E. would make our situation very disagreeable. It would expose us to an enemy's coast, the angular position of which to the Northward and Westward makes it necessary to avoid that part by standing to the Eastward. We could only lay the coast along and of course afford no drift or leeway. The horrors of shipwreck added to irretrievable slavery makes the coast very dangerous in the winter. If any cruises on this coast in a heavy gale on shore, they have no other safety but their sails, and if they once lose them, they lose all hopes of a retreat."

To guard against being trapped, Preble's first move was to safeguard his supply route through the narrow Straits of Gibraltar. He did this by appearing in force before Morocco and exacting a lasting treaty from the Emperor. Preble's ultimatum left no room for quibbling. He notified the American consul in Tangier:

"*U.S.S. Constitution*, Tangier Bay,
"Six P.M. Oct. 4, 1803

"I am honored with your communication of this evening. I shall not send a boat on shore until I have the Emperor's permission, but shall wait your communication by a shore boat.

"As you think it will gratify his Imperial Majesty, I shall salute him and dress ship; and if he is not disposed to be pacific, <u>I will salute him again.</u>

"Respectfully,
"E. Preble."

Preble had no intention of waiting for a formal declaration of war by his government if the Emperor refused. His ships were ready for action; the men were sleeping beside their guns. But the quick signing of a treaty with only minor mutual concessions and no payment of tribute secured his communications route. On November 20,

PREBLE'S SEA—*Commodore Edward Preble of* Constitution *led his squadron into the Mediterranean in 1803 to end three centuries of plundering by the piratical Barbary States. Preble's first move was to extract a treaty from the Emperor of Morocco at Tangier (1), which guaranteed him free use of the narrow Straits of Gibraltar (2). The other pirate states strung along the North African Coast were Algiers (3), Tunis (4), and Tripoli (5). Preble established his base at Syracuse (6). This chart, published in London in May of 1794, might well have been used in the operations.*

Preble declared Tripoli blockaded. He was in the process of establishing a base at Syracuse, on the island of Sicily, when he learned of the loss of the frigate *Philadelphia*. This was the greatest reverse suffered in the entire campaign, because she represented approximately a third of the squadron's power. Preble had left *Philadelphia* and some other vessels patrolling Tripoli and in his absence Captain Bainbridge ventured too close to the treacherous harbor; *Philadelphia* had run into uncharted rocks.

Philadelphia's guns could not be brought to bear on a fleet of attacking Tripolitan gunboats.

BOMBARDMENT—*Preble's squadron assaulted the pirate stronghold at Tripoli on August 3, 1804. The loss of* Philadelphia *left him with only one heavily armed three-masted vessel, his flagship* Constitution. *She is shown approaching the fortifications with an assorted squadron. From left to right are* Enterprise, Nautilus, Argus, Siren, *and* Vixen, *ranging in armament from twelve to sixteen guns; a mortar boat, a gunboat,* Constitution, *another mortar boat, and another gunboat at extreme right. Stephen Decatur directed the three gunboats in the center background. The fourth gunboat close to shore was commanded by his brother James, the only officer killed in the attack.*

She surrendered and her crew of more than three hundred officers and men began many months of enslavement. A few days later, a storm brought an unusually high tide which lifted *Philadelphia* off the reef and she became, briefly, an important addition to the Dey's forces. Officially, Bainbridge was held blameless for the loss, but he was severely criticized in some quarters.

Constitution went to her base at Syracuse, where one of the most hazardous exploits in naval history was carefully and secretly planned. A small Tripolitan trading ketch which had been captured and renamed *Intrepid* was fitted out. Stephen Decatur, one of Preble's "boys," was given the mission of entering Tripoli Harbor and burning *Philadelphia*. Decatur had volunteered for the undertaking, intending to use his own 12-gun *Enterprise,* but it was decided *Intrepid* was less likely to attract attention. Her crew of approximately seventy-five were all volunteers. The majority were from *Enterprise* plus five midshipmen from *Constitution* and a Maltese pilot, Salvadore Catalano, who later became a sailing master in the U. S. Navy.

After a series of delays caused by foul weather,

Intrepid appeared before Tripoli at dusk the night of February 16, 1804, and in the dim light of a new moon crept cautiously up the harbor. Only enough men to handle the little ketch were visible, their shipmates remaining below the bulwarks.

As *Intrepid* approached, Catalano identified her as a Maltese trader that had lost her anchors in a storm and asked permission to tie up alongside *Philadelphia*. The Moors discovered the deception too late. The Americans already were swarming aboard the frigate and corsairs leaped into the sea to escape. Each of the boarders knew his part well and within twenty minutes their firebrands had *Philadelphia* blazing from stem to stern. The flames literally drove the raiders back to *Intrepid*.

With the entire port alerted, *Intrepid's* departure was far more hazardous than her arrival. Her crew churned the water to froth with the ketch's sixteen long oars as they ran a gauntlet of gunfire from shore batteries and surrounding Tripolitan gunboats. Not the least of the din was caused by discharge of *Philadelphia's* loaded guns as flames touched them off.

Back at Syracuse three days later, Decatur boarded *Constitution* with his report for Commodore Preble. An entry in *Constitution's* log recording destruction of "the late United States Frigate *Philadelphia*" concluded: "The business being so well planned not a man was killed or wounded on our side. The Tripolitans had 20 killed, the others made their escape by jumping overboard after the ship was afire."

Now came months of intense activity for *Constitution* during which she was at sea most of the time. The squadron's manpower totaled little more than a thousand, opposing a force estimated at twenty-five thousand. *Constitution* was supported by about fifteen vessels. Tripoli Harbor was a hornets' nest of dozens of strongly armed craft which were protected by the walled city's batteries of more than a hundred large caliber guns.

Neither the heavy odds nor his own failing health deterred Preble. Within a month, six direct assaults were made on the citadel. In the first of these, August 3, 1804, the entire American force came in to point-blank range off the westerly entrances to the harbor. A score or more Tripolitan gunboats came out to meet the attack and the Moors learned for the first time what they could expect from the U. S. Navy. *Constitution* laid down a heavy bombardment, but the fiercest fighting was hand-to-hand combat between crews of the smaller craft. A shift in the wind forced the American fleet to draw away from the dangerous lee shore but not before it inflicted heavy damage. The town panicked. A minaret was toppled, three of the Dey's gunboats were captured, and many of his men were killed or wounded.

American casualties were light by comparison and none of the ships was seriously damaged. *Constitution* suffered some injury to sails, rigging, and the foremast.

The Dey sent word he would consider negotiated terms, but since no flag of truce appeared on his castle, Preble decided to attack again on the 7th. Rough weather prevented *Constitution* from drawing close enough to bring her guns to bear and the assault was executed by the smaller vessels. Again the town was heavily damaged by gunfire but the Tripolitan vessels remained well within the harbor, sheltered by rocks.

The next attack opened the night of August 24 with the small craft again initiating the action. Because of lack of wind, they had to resort to oars. Bombardment continued until dawn, but little damage was inflicted.

The assault was resumed four nights later with the smaller vessels again in the lead. They gained a position close to the rocks and bombarded every available target. They withdrew at dawn and *Constitution* moved in alone. Preble's report to the Secretary of the Navy describes the action, although it makes only slight reference to the heavy fire from shore batteries:

"We continued running in, until we were within musket shot of the Crown and Mole batteries, when we brought to, and fired upwards of three hundred round shot, besides grape and cannister, into the town, Bashaw's castle, and batteries. We silenced the castle and two of the batteries for some time. At a quarter past six, the gunboats being all out of shot and in tow, I hauled off, after having been three quarters of an hour in close action. The gunboats fired upwards of four hundred round shot, besides grape and cannister, with good effect. A large Tunisian galliot was sunk in the mole—a Spanish Seignoir received considerable damage. The Tripoline galleys and gunboats lost many men and were much cut."

Constitution also suffered battle damage but not enough to cripple her, and Preble prepared for a fifth assault against the pirate stronghold. This was carried out September 3 with *Constitution* firing eleven broadsides into the town and shore batteries. Then the wind shifted and the squadron was compelled to withdraw.

Action against the corsairs ended the next night on a mysterious and tragic note. *Intrepid,* which served Decatur in burning *Philadelphia,* had been prepared as a fire ship, laden with a hundred barrels of powder. She was guided into the harbor by Captain Richard Somers of *Nautilus* and other volunteers. It was hoped disaster would be inflicted on the enemy's fleet, but she and her crew vanished in the blinding flash of a premature explosion. The tremendous blast

did cause considerable damage, but *Intrepid* had not reached the main concentration of shipping.

The squadron was due for another disappointment. On September 10, the frigates *President* and *Constellation* arrived with Commodore Samuel Barron to take over command. The relief of Preble was not a reflection on him, but he and his command felt it keenly. Officially, he was highly commended, but many felt he was shabbily treated after he had drubbed the corsairs into submission, leaving little for successors to do but conclude treaties ending their plunders.

Preble may have been unpopular when he came aboard, but as he departed all *Constitution's* officers were moved to sign a letter telling him of their regret.

During his command no man had been killed while aboard and only one wounded, a marine, although on occasion grape shot was found imbedded in *Constitution's* stout planking. Preble came home on the frigate *John Adams.* The corsairs had been well softened when Preble was relieved and his successors were not again called on to use *Constitution's* guns to obtain acceptable agreements. Barron's arrival with four additional frigates and the capture of a corsair stronghold at Derne by a land force under General William Eaton greatly strengthened the American position. Preble had proven the power the Yankees could exert from the sea. The Dey of Tripoli now was ready for peace.

Illness caused Commodore Barron to turn over the command of the Mediterranean squadron to Commodore John Rodgers, who lost no time in demanding a showdown from the Dey. A treaty was drawn in *Constitution's* cabin, signed in June 1805, under which $60,000 was paid for release of American captives but which called for no further tribute.

His greed whetted by Tripoli's success in extorting large sums of money, the ruler of neighboring Tunis, the Bey, indicated he, too, felt entitled to raid the U. S. Treasury. Rodgers thought differently, and on August 1 anchored most of his force off Tunis. His method was very similar to that used by Preble in bringing

AN AVENGING BROTHER—*James Decatur was shot through the head by the captain of a Tripolitan vessel which had feigned surrender. His brother, Stephen, the hero of the burning of* Philadelphia, *pursued, boarded, and captured the Tripolitan craft. It is reported that in the raging free-for-all which followed, Stephen's sword was broken and one of his own men charged in and saved him from a death blow. This is a romanticized version of the hand-to-hand battle.*

FROM THE SHORES OF TRIPOLI · 1804

Morocco to terms at the start of the campaign. Rodgers sent the American Consul General the following ultimatum:

"He [the Bey] must do one of three things, by simple request, or else do all three by force. He must give the guarantee already required—or, he must give sufficient security for peace and send a minister to the United States—or, he must make such alterations in the treaty as you may require, and as may satisfy you that there is confidence to be placed in what he does.

"I have only to repeat, that if he does not do all that is necessary and proper, at the risk of my conduct being disapproved by my country, he shall feel the vengeance of the squadron now in the bay."

A treaty was promptly signed ending any demand for payment of tribute to Tunis.

Constitution remained on the Mediterranean station until 1807 to guarantee continued good behavior by the commerce raiders. Then she came home to spend two years at the New York Navy Yard. Several calmer voyages followed, including transport of some of our diplomatic agents to foreign posts.

Under command of Captain Isaac Hull, she returned to the United States and underwent considerable repair at the Washington Navy Yard, which put her in excellent condition for the War of 1812.

On one of her earlier visits to Gibraltar she had been in company with a Yankee brig, and had greatly impressed England's great sea lord, Horatio Nelson, who observed *Constitution* and those who handled her so smartly. He said:

"In the handling of those trans-Atlantic ships there is a nucleus of trouble for the Navy of Great Britain."

In 1803, Napoleon had anticipated Britain's troubles with the Americans. After signing the agreement for the Louisiana Purchase he said:

"I have this day given Britain a maritime rival who will sooner or later humble her pride."

One of the country's most important gains in the Barbary campaign was that it provided the Navy with a seasoned corps of highly proficient young officers. Many of those who won fame during the War of 1812 had their training in Preble's off-shore school. These officers were proud to be known as "Preble's 'boys.'"

"TO THE SHORES OF TRIPOLI"— *Capture of the grim fortification at Derne inspired the line in the Marine Corps anthem. It was taken April 26, 1805, by an overland expedition led by General William Eaton, which marched six hundred miles across the desert from Alexandria. The force included a detail of Marines under Lieutenant Presley O'Bannon and had support from the guns of three ships of Preble's old squadron. Eaton was severely wounded in the assault and O'Bannon took command. The Tripolitan banner was hauled down and for the first time in the country's history the flag of the United States was raised over a fortress of the Old World.*

"WHITE ASH BREEZE"—*Constitution had scarcely begun her first cruise in the War of 1812 when she was almost trapped by a five-ship British squadron. The wind was so light that all the ships lost steerageway when Constitution was just beyond the range of enemy guns. Skill, resourcefulness, and back-breaking toil by Captain Isaac Hull and his crew saved her. First an attempt was made to keep Constitution out of harm's way by resorting to a "white ash breeze"—oars—and towing her with the ship's boats. Then an anchor was carried out ahead, dropped, and Constitution was hauled up to it. The British promptly adopted the Yankee tactics and in a three-day slow-motion chase Constitution's crew had little food or rest. She finally made good her escape when Hull out-foxed the British in a rain squall: as the storm approached Constitution, Hull had her sails hastily taken in; the alarmed British followed suit. But Hull's seeming caution was a trick. As soon as Constitution was hidden by the rain he immediately reset all her sails. She was away at an eleven-knot clip.*

Escape

There was little reason for optimism when Congress declared war on Britain on June 18, 1812. The new Navy had only a score of warships. The Royal Navy had six to seven hundred armed vessels, including numerous line-of-battle ships. The United States had no ships of this size and could not afford combat with the enemy's more powerful warships. Many of England's ships were engaged in fighting a bitter war with France, but this did not cancel a great difference between the two navies.

Although *Constitution* is best known for victories, one of her escapes must be considered almost as important as any single battle. Only a month after the declaration of war, she escaped from a squadron of five British warships which together mounted well over two hundred guns against the fifty-five *Constitution* probably carried at the time. Skill, daring, and the most demanding labor made possible her continued life and later victories.

Constitution was bound up the coast from Chesapeake Bay for New York where Captain Isaac Hull expected to join the squadron of Commodore John Rodgers. Instead, there was a very confused meeting with the British ships off the New Jersey shore on July 17. Hull at first mistook them for Rodgers' squadron, and the British commanders also had difficulty separating friend from foe. The British vessels, under Commodore P. V. B. Broke, were the 64-gun ship *Africa*, 38-gun frigates *Shannon* and *Belvidera*, 32-gun frigate *Aeolus* and the 38-gun frigate *Guerriere*, last to join the rendezvous.

The light breeze dropped to a flat calm at nightfall and left the six ships scattered and drifting aimlessly on a glassy sea. Dawn, however, brought recognition, and a chase immediately started with *Constitution* as the lone quarry. Shots were exchanged but caused little damage. The wind continued too light to furnish steerageway and finally the belligerents resorted to the oars of their ships' boats which were pressed into service to propel the warships. But with the enemy gaining, Hull prepared to make a stand and go down fighting. He later gave his first lieutenant, Charles Morris, full credit for a suggestion which probably saved *Constitution*—use of a kedge anchor. A member of the crew described the operation. In his pamphlet, "Naval Scenes In the Last War," one of *Constitution's* crew members, gunner Moses Smith, reported:

"Captain Hull came aft, cooly surveyed the scene, took a match in his hand, and ordered the quarter-master to hoist the American flag. I stood within a few feet of Hull at the time. He clapped the fire to my gun, No. 1, and such a barking as sounded over the sea! It was worth hearing. No sooner had our iron dog opened his mouth in this manner, than the whole enemy opened the whole of theirs. Every one of the ships fired directly toward us. Those nearest kept up their firing for some time; but of course not a shot reached us then, at the distance we were.

63

"Captain Hull gave up the match to the captain of the gun, and we kept blazing away with our stern chasers. The shots we fired helped send us ahead, out of the reach of the enemy. There was little or no wind; but we resolved to save ourselves from capture, or sink in the conflict. We soon found, however, that we made but slow work in getting ahead.

"Hull called Lieutenant Morris to him and said calmly, 'Let's lay broadside to them, Mr. Morris, and fight the whole! If they sink us, we'll go down like men!'

"We were off Little Egg Harbour, on the New Jersey shore, at the time stretching in toward the Delaware Bay. The enemy had drawn in between us and the land so that the prospect was they might cut us off from the Capes.

"Mr. Morris now spoke to Captain Hull: 'There is one thing, sir, I think we'd better try.'

" 'What's that?' replied Hull.

" 'Try to kedge her off,' [a method for moving a ship by carrying out an anchor and then drawing the vessel up to it] said the lieutenant."

All available cordage was joined to the anchor cable and two ship's boats carried the anchor out ahead of *Constitution*. Accounts vary as to the anchors used. They were either sea anchors or small ship's anchors. (A sea anchor resembles a large umbrella made of canvas stretched over wooden ribs.) The sea-anchor version seems more plausible. The back-breaking task of hauling in the cable was repeated throughout the night, with all hands working. Although the British soon imitated the procedure, *Constitution* was still out of range at dawn, and when a breeze sprang up, *Constitution* left her pursuers to leeward and ended the three days of peril.

The escape astonished the British commanders, who scarcely could have been more chagrined if they had lost one of their own ships.

Not wishing to risk meeting blockading forces off New York, Hull shaped a course for Boston, arriving after twenty-two days at sea. There he issued a statement requesting that plaudits directed to him be distributed among his "brave officers and crew." The statement concluded:

"Captain Hull has great pleasure in saying, that notwithstanding the length of the chase, and the officers and crew being deprived of sleep, and allowed but little refreshment during the time, not a murmur was heard to escape them."

Guerriere

If Captain Isaac Hull had waited for orders, *Constitution* might never have scored her most celebrated victory over the British frigate *Guerriere.*

When *Constitution* returned to Boston after the fox-and-hounds chase with Broke's squadron, Hull's orders had not arrived. Hull knew he was risking his naval career but he felt it wiser to get to sea than be trapped by a British blockade. Ironically, when the orders did reach Boston they read to remain in port.

Constitution sailed from Boston August 2, 1812, and on the 19th found *Guerriere* some six hundred miles to the eastward. The ships sighted each other about two in the afternoon, but Hull had no notion of following the British doctrine of naval warfare laid down by Lord Nelson—"Never mind manoeuvres, always go at them." Instead, he made careful preparations and kept a favorable windward position until he was satisfied it was time to close with the enemy. *Guerriere,* which the British had captured from the French in 1806, was under the command of Captain James Dacres.

Moses Smith, describing the meeting with *Guerriere,* wrote:

"Before all hands could be called, there was a general rush on deck. The word passed like lightning from man to man; and all who could be spared, came flocking up like pigeons from a net bed. From the spar deck to the gun deck, from that to the berth deck, every man was roused and on his feet. All eyes were turned in the direction of the strange sail, and quick as thought, studding-sails were out, fore and aft. The noble frigate fairly bounded over the billows, as we gave her a rap full, and spread her broad and tall wings to the gale.

"The stranger hauled his wind, and laid to for us. It was evident that he was an English man-of-war of a large class and all ready for action. . . .

"As we came up she began to fire. They were evidently trying to rake us. But we continued on our course, tacking and half-tacking, taking good care to avoid being raked. We came so near on one tack, that an eighteen-pound shot came through us under the larboard [port] knight-head, striking just abaft the breech of the gun to which I belonged. The splinters flew in all directions; but no one was hurt. We immediately picked up the shot, and put it in the mouth of long Tom, a large gun loose on deck—and sent it home again, with our respects.

"Another stray shot hit our foremast, cutting one of the hoops in two. But the mast was not otherwise injured, and the slight damage was soon repaired.

"Hull was now all animation. He saw that the decisive moment had come. With great energy, yet calmness of manner, he passed around among the officers and men, addressing to them words of confidence and encouragement.

"'Men,' said he, 'now do your duty. Your officers cannot have entire command over you now. Each man must do all in his power for his country.'"

DRAMA ON THE HIGH SEAS—
Only one month after Constitution *eluded the British squadron, she found* Guerriere, *one of her recent pursuers, some six hundred miles east of Boston. The series of paintings by Thomas Birch (above and on the following two pages) graphically depicts phases of the meeting. Here, Constitution's men are aloft and on the bowsprit shortening sail in preparation for the impending battle. The originals of this series are the property of the United States Naval Academy. President John Fitzgerald Kennedy borrowed them to hang in his White House office.*

67

As Hull maneuvered to bring the guns to bear, he told the impatient crew:

"You shall have her as close as you please. Sailing master! lay her alongside!"

A devastating broadside from guns double-shotted with round and grape swept *Guerriere*. The two ships engaged in a furious exchange with the British firing more rapidly but with little accuracy. Much of *Guerriere's* fire went into *Constitution's* rigging. *Constitution* concentrated on her foe's hull. *Guerriere's* mizzen-mast was shot away within fifteen minutes of Hull's first broadside.

After surging ahead of *Guerriere*, Hull brought *Constitution* about, intending to cross her bow to rake the enemy ship, but because of damage to her rigging, *Constitution* was difficult to manage. As a result, *Guerriere* drove her bowsprit and jib boom into *Constitution's* mizzen rigging. As the ships drew apart, *Guerriere's* fore- and mainmasts also came crashing down, leaving her a helpless, wallowing wreck. Efforts of her crew to get her under control were futile, and

"OLD IRONSIDES"—*Above*, Constitution *ranges alongside and, keeping her fire low, inflicts devastating injury to* Guerriere's *hull. The foe's mizzen-mast was shot away almost at the outset of the battle.*

Above right, the antagonists crash together in heavy seas with Guerriere's *bowsprit flailing* Constitution's *quarter-deck. As the two ships draw apart,* Guerriere's *shattered fore- and mainmasts also go by the board.*

Below right, Guerriere *is a dismasted, helpless hulk after* Constitution's *most celebrated victory, from which she emerged without critical damage. A Yankee gunner who saw a shot bounce off* Constitution's *oaken planking shouted: "Her sides are made of iron!" Thus she earned the name by which she is best known to millions—Old Ironsides.*

68

after *Constitution* made emergency repairs and again approached her, *Guerriere* fired a gun to leeward in token of surrender.

At the height of this engagement *Constitution* earned the nickname by which she became best known to generations of Americans—Old Ironsides. According to legend, a gunner aboard *Constitution* saw a British shot bounce off her oaken planking and exclaimed: "Her sides are made of iron!"

Deeds of daring were commonplace, but the Navy commemorated one in 1919 by naming a destroyer in memory of an Irish lad named Daniel Hogan, who served during this battle as an ordinary seaman:

"During the engagement with the British frigate *Guerriere*, when the flag was shot away from the foretop-gallant masthead, he climbed up and lashed it in place in the face of the firing."

When the battle was over, a boarding party from *Constitution* saw that *Guerriere* was too badly damaged to be brought home as a prize, so the 267 survivors were taken aboard *Constitution*. At Hull's orders *Guerriere* was set afire

and she disappeared in a tremendous explosion when flames reached her magazines.

Constitution had proved herself superior to her foe in every respect. While records were not kept with any uniformity it is surmised that she carried fifty-five guns and could deliver a broadside of 684 pounds. *Guerriere* is believed to have carried forty-nine guns, with a broadside potential of 556 pounds. *Constitution* is believed to have carried a crew of 456, of whom seven were killed, one accidentally by the misfire of one of her own guns. Her displacement was given at 1,576 tons. *Guerriere's* crew was listed at 282, fifteen of whom were killed, and her displacement at 1,338 tons.

Constitution returned to Boston with her prisoners on August 30, 1812, and was given an exuberant welcome—the victory gave a much-needed lift to the country whose battles ashore were not going well.

The return also brought a change in command. Hull, after two years, turned the command of Old Ironsides over to his friend Commodore William Bainbridge.

70

A HARD-WON WAGER—*In a cordial meeting before the war, the Captains Hull and Dacres had wagered a hat on the outcome if* Constitution *ever met* Guerriere *in combat. It is reported that they engaged in the following exchange when Dacres came aboard as a prisoner from the helpless wreck of* Guerriere, *left.*

"Dacres, my dear fellow, I am glad to see you on board," said Hull, advancing and offering his hand.

"D--n it, Hull," responded Dacres, "I suppose you are"; and, unbuckling his sword, he offered it to his captor.

"I will not take a sword from one who knows so well how to use it," said Captain Hull; "but, I tell you, Dacres, I will trouble you for that hat."

THE SPIRIT OF 1812—Constitution's *men had the best of reasons for enthusiasm. They fought not only for ship and country but for freedom on the high seas. This old print shows a gun crew at its station during the battle with* Guerriere, *jubilant over the striking of a telling blow. But the young boy who carried the explosives, the powder monkey, is not diverted as he speeds to feed the loud-mouthed iron dog. This defeat of a British ship had great significance for both sides: it did much to dispel the illusion that the British Navy was invincible, and it brought confidence to both the young American Navy and the nation.*

Java

Constitution's crew was so openly dissatisfied when Commodore William Bainbridge succeeded Isaac Hull as commanding officer that some of the more outspoken were ordered off the ship to other duty. Disappointment over losing Hull had something to do with the crew's discontent. Furthermore, Bainbridge was known as a stern disciplinarian with his men.

Old Ironsides left Boston on October 27, 1812, for the West Indies, and a record of numerous punishments indicates that she was not a happy ship. Her triumph over the British frigate *Java* improved morale.

Constitution encountered *Java* off the Brazilian coast the morning of December 29. The battle which followed paralleled, in some respects, Hull's victory over *Guerriere. Java's* firepower was slightly greater than *Guerriere's.* She was faster and carried many more men, probably over four hundred, since she had a considerable number aboard enroute to duty elsewhere. *Java* had been captured from the French and, like *Guerriere,* was considered better than most British frigates of the same class.

Constitution drew *Java* away from the coast to gain sea room in which to fight. It was well into the afternoon before Bainbridge felt he was a sufficient distance from shore. He turned, headed straight for *Java,* and fired an opening broadside from almost the maximum range of *Constitution's* long 24-pounders. The Commodore's strategy was to weaken *Java* as much as possible with long guns before coming within

range of the foe's carronades. *Java* repeatedly tried to cross *Constitution's* bow to rake her and as many times was treated to a broadside from Old Ironsides before she tacked away in a screen of powder smoke. *Java* was unsuccessful, too, in attempts to board her enemy.

Within an hour, all *Java's* spars were shot away. Commodore Bainbridge's journal furnishes this account:

"At forty minutes past two, determined to close with the enemy notwithstanding his raking. Set the fore-and mainsail and luffed up close to him. At fifty minutes past two the enemy's jib-boom got foul of our mizzen rigging. At three the head of the enemy's bowsprit and jib-boom were shot away by us. At five minutes past three, shot away the enemy's foremast by the board. At fifteen minutes past three, shot away his main top mast just above the cap. At forty minutes past three, shot away the gaff and spanker boom. At fifty-five minutes past three, shot away his mizzenmast nearly by the board."

Of *Java's* spars, only a stub of the mainmast remained, and fallen wreckage made it impossible to man most of her guns. *Constitution* drew away and made temporary repairs while, aboard *Java,* a futile attempt was being made to restore her to fighting trim. But her condition was hopeless, and, when *Constitution* approached, *Java* struck her colors. About fifty of her crew were dead or dying and about a hundred had been wounded. Her commander, Captain Henry Lambert, died soon after reaching shore.

Constitution had lost twelve men and twenty-two were wounded, including Bainbridge.

Examination showed that, as with *Guerriere,* there was no hope of bringing *Java* home as a prize. After survivors were taken off, she was set afire; like *Guerriere,* the explosion of her magazines sank her. The prisoners were landed at Sao Salvador (Bahai), on the coast of Brazil, and Old Ironsides returned to Boston, her home port, the last day of February 1813 to another victory celebration. *Constitution* went to the Boston Navy Yard for a needed overhaul.

Before relinquishing command to become commander of the Yard, Bainbridge performed a service which must have done much to win favor with the crew. Prize money had been voted by Congress for the destruction of *Guerriere* but never received, and an additional award of $50,000 was made for destroying *Java.* Bainbridge prodded the government, and both awards were promptly paid.

The victories caused consternation in England while stirring the United States Congress to authorize, belatedly, four new line-of-battle ships and six frigates. The war ended before they got to sea, and our dwindling fleet saw it to a close.

It was said in some quarters that the American frigates were ships-of-the-line in disguise and that this gave them an unfair military advantage. Britishers who protested that introduction of the new frigates was not altogether sporting—not quite cricket, perhaps—failed to consider other factors. The American victories also represented superior gunnery, sail-handling, and strategy by eager sailormen who had volunteered their services to their country. Previous hostile acts by the Barbary pirates, France, and England had idled numerous American merchant ships making many experienced seamen available for naval duty. Before the war ended, England attempted to build new frigates and cut down line-of-battle ships in the hope of meeting our frigates on more equal terms.

Naval victories counteracted the discouragement caused by numerous reverses in the war ashore.

FIERCEST FRIGATE ACTION OF THE WAR—Constitution *reduced* Java *to a lumbering hulk through the same deliberate method used to dispose of* Guerriere. *The illustrations, particularly those inserted in the sailing diagram, clearly show damage to* Constitution *sails; British gunners kept their fire high, while the Yankees probed for the heart of their quarry in the hull itself.* Constitution *emerged damaged but not out of control, while* Java *was so badly injured she could not be brought home as a prize. Before the battle ended,* Constitution *had shot away all of* Java's *spars. The defeat of* Java *caused the British Admiralty to issue orders that their frigates were not to engage the 44-gun American frigates in any single action.*

Time – 2 O'Clock & 50 min. P.M.

Time – 4 O'Clock & 25 min. P.M.
CLOSING SCENE.

Wind – N.E.

Time – 2 O'Clock 10 min. P.M.

Java   Constitution

USS CONSTITUTION DEFEATS *HMS JAVA*
December 29, 1812

Cyane — Levant

Under Captain Charles Stewart, who had succeeded Commodore Bainbridge, *Constitution* left Boston on the last day of 1813 to raid British commerce. In three months at sea, she took only a few merchant prizes and destroyed the 14-gun *Pictou* before heading home.

Old Ironsides' career almost ended within sight of her home port of Boston at the conclusion of this cruise.

It had been Stewart's intention to put in at Portsmouth, New Hampshire, but a shift in wind made this impossible and a course was set for Boston. On April 3, 1814, *Constitution* worked down the coast in a light breeze which fell to a flat calm just as two 38-gun British frigates, *Tenedos* and *Junon*, bore down on her taking advantage of a brisk breeze which had not reached *Constitution*. Having passed Cape Ann and Gloucester Harbor, she was pinned against Massachusetts' rocky North Shore with escape by sea cut off. Stewart wanted to seek refuge in Salem Harbor, but no one aboard was familiar with its difficult approaches. Marblehead was the only alternative, and Stewart had to take this long chance. As the British ships continued to gain, all goods aboard that could be spared were jettisoned to lighten the ship and increase her speed. Over the side went spare spars, stores, and valuable prize merchandise. The fresh water and the spirits were pumped overboard. These sacrifices paid off, for soon *Constitution* gained the security of the little harbor. There she was protected by the guns of Fort Sewall and the militia which rallied from coastal

towns. The British decided not to test the defense and sailed away. A few days later *Constitution* came down to Boston where she was blockaded eight and a half months.

She received jubilant receptions on her earlier victorious returns to her home port, but it soon became apparent some of the cheering had been by fair weather friends. Pressure was brought to have *Constitution* leave the Navy Yard and move down the harbor, where the blockading fleet could get at her without damaging the town, but this proposal that Old Ironsides become a sacrificial offering was successfully resisted. Finally, on December 18, 1814, while winter weather disrupted the blockade, Stewart slipped *Constitution* out of the harbor and clear of the land.

This was *Constitution's* last war cruise.

She took two British merchantmen, but the voyage was otherwise uneventful until February 20, 1815, when the 34-gun frigate *Cyane* and the 20-gun sloop *Levant* were sighted and pursued off the Madeira Islands.

The meeting was late in the afternoon. Maneuvers of the British commanders, Captain Gordon Falcon of *Cyane* and Captain the Honorable George Douglass of *Levant*, indicated they wished to delay action in hope of a better opportunity to disable *Constitution* in darkness.

Stewart had other plans, and the engagement opened as the sun set. Broadsides were exchanged with *Cyane*, about three hundred yards to leeward, and hot action developed. The moon appeared but visibility was reduced by mist and gunsmoke. *Constitution* drew abeam of *Levant* and belted her with a broadside as *Cyane* came up astern intending to rake *Constitution*. Then Stewart executed a difficult piece of sail-handling: he backed *Constitution* down, poured heavy fire into *Cyane*, and hit *Levant* with two additional broadsides. *Levant* was forced to drop out of the fray temporarily. *Cyane* tried to run off before the wind, but *Constitution* raked her over the stern. Hopelessly crippled *Cyane* surrendered, forty minutes after the engagement opened. *Levant* tried to get back into the engagement alone, but she was quickly overpowered by Old Ironsides.

Stewart's skill in handling *Constitution* had enabled her to wear down *Cyane* and *Levant*

THE CURTAIN COMES DOWN— Constitution *fought her last battle under the command of Captain Charles Stewart near the Madeira Islands off the African coast. There she encountered the British frigate* Cyane *and the sloop-of-war* Levant *on February 20, 1815.* Constitution *whittled down the strength of each separately.* Cyane *was subdued first.* Levant *withdrew from the action long enough to repair her rigging and returned to the fray, but* Cyane *had already struck her colors; after a quick exchange of gunfire,* Levant *was persuaded to surrender.*

AFTER THE BATTLE—*Constitution takes battered* Cyane *in tow for haven in a neutral port. Although the island port reached was neutral, Stewart did not feel secure there and, on March 10, 1815, when several large ships approached through the fog, he ordered the anchor cables cut.* Constitution *and the two prizes fled to sea. An unsuccessful chase by three frigates of Captain Sir George Collier's squadron was described in the "Naval History of Great Britain," published in London in 1837, as "...the most blundering piece of business recorded in these six volumes."*

without having had to take their combined fire simultaneously. *Cyane* and *Levant* had a total of 763 pounds of metal in their combined broadsides, compared with *Constitution's* 704.

Of *Constitution's* crew of 451, six were killed and nine wounded. Between *Cyane* and *Levant,* with crews totaling 320, nineteen were killed and forty-two wounded. *Cyane* suffered thirty-eight casualties from her complement of 180. *Levant's* casualties were twenty-three of 140.

After putting the three ships in order, *Constitution* sailed with *Cyane* and *Levant* for the Cape Verde Islands off the African coast to land prisoners. On March 10, while at Port Praya, her career almost ended: the sails of a large ship suddenly appeared over low-lying fog outside, then the sails of two other ships. Stewart ordered

Constitution's anchor cable cut and directed his prize crews to get *Cyane* and *Levant* underway immediately. The three vessels cleared the harbor and a baffling chase began. All that was visible to the crews were the upper sails of the mystery ships above the fog. Stewart's suspicions about the strangers were confirmed by English prisoners still aboard. They identified them as units of Captain Sir George Collier's squadron—the 50-gun frigates *Leander* and *Newcastle* and the 40-gun *Acasta*. *Leander* and *Newcastle* had been designed and built to excel the new class of American frigates. Collier's force had been seeking *Constitution* ever since she had eluded his blockade at Boston.

As the chase grew hot, there was some gunfire that fell short of *Constitution.* Old Ironsides' superior speed stood her in good stead, and she pursued an uneventful voyage home, by way of the West Indies, arriving in New York on May 15, 1815. *Cyane,* making a direct crossing, preceded her and had been added to our forces. *Levant* had been chased back to Port Praya, a neutral port, where she was attacked by *Newcastle* and *Acasta* although she signaled surrender. British embarrassment over permitting *Constitution* to escape was not lessened by discovery that *Levant* was not another American frigate but one of their own small vessels previously taken as a prize. Stewart's log noted:

"It became necessary to separate from the *Levant* or to risk being brought into action to cover her. . . . The whole of the enemy's squadron tacked in pursuit of the *Levant* and gave over the pursuit of this ship. . . . This sacrifice of the *Levant* became necessary for the preservation of the *Constitution.*"

It is worth noting that had effective communications systems been in operation, *Constitution's* last battle would not have been fought. In the *Cyane-Levant* engagement on February 20, 1815, both sides were aware peace was near if not actually agreed upon. But in the absence of reliable information from home offices, the opposing commanders were called upon to make their own decisions and they chose, without apparent reluctance, to fight. In fact, a peace treaty already had been signed at Ghent on December 24, 1814, and ratified by the United States on February 17, 1815. The terms allowed thirty days for word to reach distant commands and end hostilities, which legalized Old Ironsides' victory. Andrew Jackson's triumph over Major General Sir Edward Pakenham at New Orleans was scored under similar circumstances on January 8, 1815.

So ended the War of 1812. The hard-fought naval engagements closed not in bitterness but in mutual respect between the opposing forces. During the war, proposals were made for meetings of evenly matched ships, but the United States could not afford to make war a sporting event. Such balanced contests were too likely to bring equal losses and expend the American's ships before the enemy's.

When, earlier in the war, *Guerriere* surrendered and her wounded commander came aboard *Constitution* as a prisoner, Isaac Hull helped him over the side and declined Captain Dacres' proffered sword. In reporting, Dacres told his superiors:

"I feel it my duty to state that conduct of Captain Hull and his officers to our men has been that of a brave enemy; the greatest care being taken to prevent our men losing the smallest trifle and the greatest attention being paid to the wounded."

The surrender of *Java's* commander, Captain Lambert, was more tragic. He died of his wounds shortly after being taken ashore in Brazil. As Lambert was leaving *Constitution,* Commodore Bainbridge, severely wounded himself, was assisted on deck for a parting courtesy and to return Lambert's sword.

Lieutenant Henry Chads, who succeeded to command when Lambert was wounded, reported to the British Admiralty ". . .grateful acknowledgement for the generous treatment Captain Lambert and his officers have experienced from our gallant enemy." Later he was quoted as saying *Constitution* was handled so skillfully ". . .it made me regret that she was not British."

Quiet Years

Constitution came home from the wars in 1815 too sea-worn and battered to participate in a bit of unfinished business with the Algerian corsairs. While our ships were occupied with the War of 1812, the Algerians seized the opportunity to again attack our merchant ships. Two squadrons were sent to the Mediterranean, one under Commodore Stephen Decatur and the other under Commodore William Bainbridge, and the remaining Barbary pirates were subdued.

Old Ironsides remained idle six years, during which she underwent extensive repairs. Then, on May 13, 1821, she departed from Boston under the command of Captain Jacob Jones to resume duty as flagship of the Mediterranean squadron. During this cruise, *Constitution* was visited by the English poet Lord Byron.

Constitution came home to Boston in 1823 to take aboard a new crew and, after refitting, returned to the Mediterranean. This four-year tour of duty consisted largely of "showing the flag" as protection for American shipping.

Upon returning to Boston, *Constitution* was withdrawn from service on July 19, 1828. After a survey, she was pronounced unseaworthy in 1830. Her planking and decking had decayed badly, although most of her timbers were sound. The Navy Department ruled she should be sold or scrapped, a decision which so outraged a young law student, Oliver Wendell Holmes, that he composed his stirring poem "Old Ironsides."

Published in newspapers throughout the country, it rolled up such a tidal wave of protest that *Constitution's* death warrant was quickly withdrawn and, instead, funds were appropriated for restoration of the old frigate. At the Boston Navy Yard, on June 24, 1833, she became the first occupant of a new drydock which bears her name to this day. The operation revealed a serious distortion of her keel. This "hogging," as much as two and a half feet, was variously attributed to difficulties experienced in her initial launching and the great burden of armament she had carried fore and aft. The distortion was corrected in restoring her to a seaworthy state. What effect it may have had on her remarkable sailing qualities could not be determined. During the repairs, *Constitution* was again under command of Isaac Hull.

80

The Decapitation of a great Blockhead by the Mysterious agency of the Claret coloured Coat.

Reconstruction no sooner was completed in 1834 than a furious storm erupted over the installation of a new figurehead representing President Andrew Jackson.

Her original figurehead represented Hercules, a symbol of strength, but it was destroyed during the Barbary wars in a collision with a sister ship. It was replaced by a purely decorative billet, or fiddlehead, so called because the tops of the timbers were carved much like the scrolls on the head of a violin. Some historians claim a figure of Neptune graced *Constitution's* prow during this period.

Jesse D. Elliott was Commandant of the Boston Navy Yard in 1833, and he decided Old Ironsides deserved something more elaborate than a billet head. He could not have anticipated the fury of objections to his choice of President Jackson as the subject of a new figurehead. Jackson had many strong political opponents in Boston at that time. Elliott was threatened with bodily harm, but, with the Navy Department's approval, he arranged to have a skilled woodcarver, Laban S. Beecher, proceed with the work. Pressure—even attempted bribery—was brought to bear on Beecher to have him quit the task or dispose of the unfinished work as the project became more and more a violent political

A FIGUREHEAD OF CONTROVERSY—*A political storm broke over* Constitution *in 1834. President Andrew Jackson's political enemies violently protested the installation of a life-sized image of "Old Hickory" as Old Ironsides' figurehead. One stormy night, a Cape Cod merchant skipper, undetected by armed sentinels, sawed off the head of the image. Jackson's friends were outraged; his foes, delighted. Eventually the figurehead was repaired. An image of President Jackson decorated Old Ironsides' prow for many years. As shown at left, the figurehead is believed to have represented Jackson in his riding habit. Above is a political cartoon published by the anti-Jackson press.*

issue. To safeguard the carving, Elliott had it removed to the Navy Yard where, with an armed guard standing by, Beecher completed it.

Some of the arguments against honoring President Jackson seem to have been reasonable. It was, at least, unusual to confer such an honor on a living person. Also, it was noted that while the President was one of the nation's most conspicuous military heroes, he had no naval experience and there were many naval heroes eligible for such an honor.

The dispute raged on but "Old Hickory's" image was installed beneath Old Ironsides' bowsprit in the spring of 1834. As added protection for the figurehead, *Constitution* was given a berth between two line-of-battle ships and armed marines were stationed on all three ships' bows, night and day. Despite these precautions, a merchant ship skipper from Cape Cod, on the night of July 2, 1834, rowed across the harbor to the Navy Yard at the height of a violent thunder storm. Undetected, Samuel W. Dewey gained a position beneath the bowsprit and, sawing furiously as thunder rolled, he severed the head and returned with it to the city.

Dewey was an adventurous mariner and it is not clear if his motive was political or prankish, but he found himself regarded as a hero by Jackson's opponents in Boston and other Eastern cities. The head was secretly displayed at many political meetings. An offer of $1,000 reward by Captain Elliott and a threat to court-martial all hands at the Navy Yard failed to recover the head. It remained officially missing until Dewey himself appeared at the office of the Secretary of the Navy some six months later to voluntarily surrender the head and tell the story. When the story reached President Jackson, he was highly amused and was reported to have said, "I never did like that image! Give the man a postmaster's job!"

Elliott covered the mutilated figurehead with canvas and waited to have the controversial figurehead repaired until he sailed to New York as *Constitution's* commander in March 1835. A likeness of "Old Hickory" adorned the frigate's bow some forty years before it was replaced with another billet head.

Constitution sailed on March 16 to bring home our Minister to France. The ship returned June 22, and Captain Elliott sailed again in August as commander-in-chief of the Mediterranean Squadron on a three-year tour of duty. On a call at the British Naval Station on the island of Malta in 1836 it was apparent old animosities between the United States and Great Britain were forgotten. The former enemy joined the American force in an observance of Washington's Birthday by dressing ship and the firing of national salutes by fourteen anchored ships.

Old Ironsides returned early in August 1838 and, upon arrival at Norfolk, Captain Elliott found trouble waiting. Many of the crew were dissatisfied and demanded their discharges, which were overdue. Captain Elliott was accused of treating his crew harshly. One charge, perhaps unique in naval annals, was that he quartered jackasses on the berth deck. He was bringing the long-eared passengers back to improve the breed in the United States. Elliot was court-martialed, convicted, and suspended from the Navy for four years.

In the spring of 1839, *Constitution* left for the South Pacific Station to spend two years cruising the west coast of South America. On her return to Norfolk she reported a very rough passage around Cape Horn.

She sailed again in the spring of 1844 on a voyage to China which eventually took her around the world during a four-year period. In 495 days at sea, Old Ironsides logged well over fifty thousand miles.

Her commander was Captain John Percival, known in the Navy as "Mad Jack" because of his volatile nature. Percival was said to have been impressed at seventeen from an American merchantman by the British and to have demonstrated such proficiency as a seaman that he served as foretop captain of Nelson's flagship *Victory* in the battle of Trafalgar. Whatever the truth of this story, Percival competently guided *Constitution* on her longest voyage.

RETURN TO THE SEA — *One of the Navy's earliest photographs, above, shows* Constitution *at the Portsmouth Navy Yard in 1858, being prepared for launching after an extensive restoration. The costumes of the two women visitors and the use of oxen as draft animals help confirm the date of this early photograph. Right, the figure of Andrew Jackson that graces her bow succeeded the original Jackson figurehead.*

SERVICE AS A TRAINING SHIP—
Constitution *was assigned to the Naval Academy at Annapolis in 1860 as a training ship. Instruction aboard the Navy's most famous warship must have been an inspiration to a new generation of midshipmen, already schooled in traditions established by a long roster of men who had served her well. A class of middies, below, receives gunnery instruction on the spar deck. If the artist's portrayal is accurate, midshipmen of that era must have been much younger than those of later years. However, it had been the practice of all navies to include many teenaged boys in their warship crews during the days of sail.*

CIVIL WAR DAYS—*The outbreak of the Civil War stirred apprehension over the safety of the venerable frigate. In 1861 she was spirited away from Annapolis to Newport, Rhode Island. The Naval Academy was also transferred to Newport, where Old Ironsides served as a training ship until 1865. Constitution was anchored off Fort Adams, right, then a formidable fortification at the entrance to Newport Harbor.*

MIDDIES LEARNING THE ROPES AT THE NAVAL SCHOOL ON BOARD THE "CONSTITUTION," ANNAPOLIS

Much of her crew was ill when she called at Singapore in February of 1845, but a former enemy proved a good friend. Commodore Henry D. Chads of a British squadron came aboard to furnish assistance. As a lieutenant, thirty-two years earlier, Chads came aboard as a prisoner after *Constitution* destroyed *Java*.

During the return voyage from the Pacific Station *Constitution* spent fifty-seven days between Manila and Honolulu, ninety-seven days between Mazatlan, on Mexico's Pacific Coast, around Cape Horn to Rio de Janeiro, and sixty-one days from that Brazilian port to Boston.

After two years in the Navy Yard, she sailed again in December of 1848 under Captain John Gwynn for the Mediterranean. It was on this cruise that a Pope visited *Constitution*. The Reverend Charles W. Lyons, S.J., President of Georgetown University, gave this account:

"In December 1848, the *Constitution* set out on a cruise that took her to the Mediterranean, where she cruised mostly along the Italian coast. At that time the Pope had left Rome because of troubled times, and was receiving shelter at the hands of the King of Naples.

"Captain Gwynn extended an invitation to the King of Naples and Pope Pius IX to visit the *Constitution*, then lying in the Bay of Naples. The invitation was accepted, and these dignitaries were rowed to her in a boat manned by the captains of the other warships in the harbour, of which there were many. . . .

"This is the first and only known instance of a sovereign pontiff being on American territory — for such was the deck of 'Old Ironsides .' "

While transporting our Consul General D. S. McCauley to Alexandria from Tripoli a son was born aboard to Mrs. McCauley. He was named Constitution Stewart McCauley to honor the ship and a former commander.

MARION.   TALLAPOOSA.   CONSTITUTION. KEARSAGE. SARATOGA. POWHATAN.   PORTSMOUTH.   MINNESOTA.

U.S. NAVAL REVIEW AT HAMPTON-ROADS VA.

THE PASSING OF SAIL—*Constitution is almost obscured by smoke from more modern warships. The stacks on the others indicate that they were propelled by steam as well as by sail. The displacement of sail by steam was stoutly opposed by many windjammer sailormen, who much preferred handling great expanses of white canvas to shoveling coal. These ships were gathered for a naval review held at Hampton-Roads, Virginia about 1877.*

The cruise ended at New York, where *Constitution* again went out of commission for two years. Recommissioned December 22, 1852, she returned to her familiar Mediterranean Station but was diverted to patrolling the West African Coast in an effort to end the slave trade. She was credited with capturing at least one slave ship. She went out of commission in 1855 at Portsmouth, New Hampshire, where she was extensively rebuilt. She was recommissioned on August 1, 1860, and sent to Annapolis for use by the Naval Academy. With the start of the Civil War, fears for her safety were raised and she was spirited away from Annapolis on April 26, 1861, under tow to New York. The Naval Academy was moved to Newport, Rhode Island, and *Constitution* went along as a training ship. After the war, in 1865, *Constitution* was ordered back to Annapolis and on that voyage was able to make better time, under her own sail, than the tug assigned to tow her. She was logged at thirteen and a half knots, believed to have been her maximum speed.

Constitution began a period of inactivity dur-

86

IN DOWDY GARB—Constitution *was brought to Boston in 1897 for observance of her 100th anniversary. She had been serving as a receiving ship at Portsmouth, New Hampshire. In performance of that duty, her fine lines were hidden by a barracks structure more suggestive of a farm building than anything nautical.*

ing which the duties of her commanding officers were little more than those of ship-keepers. One, then a lieutenant commander, went on to great fame, as Admiral George Dewey.

The old frigate was found to be in a state of critical disrepair in 1871 and taken to the Philadelphia Shipyard for extensive restoration. Again seaworthy, she was recommissioned in 1877 and sailed March 4, 1878, with a cargo of merchandise for exhibition at the Universal Exposition at Paris. She sailed from Havre on January 16, 1879, to bring home the exhibits, arriving at New York on May 24 after two mishaps: she ran aground on the English coast—the British Navy sent a warship to assist her to deep water—and had trouble with her rudder, which was repaired at Lisbon, Portugal.

The next two years were spent cruising the Atlantic as a training ship for apprentices. This ended her career of sailing the high seas. She was tied up another two years at New York before being towed to Portsmouth Navy Yard as a receiving ship. John F. Fitzgerald, the maternal grandfather of President John F. Kennedy, went to Portsmouth to investigate reports that she was in danger of sinking at her pier. Fitzgerald then was a congressman from Massachusetts. An article he wrote years later reported:

"I went to Portsmouth and found the facts as related in the newspaper practically true. Returning to Washington I immediately waited upon John D. Long, former Governor of Massachusetts, who was then Secretary of the Navy, and told him that unless the government did

something the old frigate *Constitution* would soon be at the bottom of Portsmouth Harbor.

"Mr. Long asked me to see the Chief of Construction Department, Philip Hichborn. . . .

"I told them both that the *Constitution* would celebrate the 100th anniversary of her building in the fall of 1897 and it would be a fine thing to repair the ship and bring her to the Charlestown [Boston] Navy Yard, right opposite the spot where she was built 100 years before and that I would see the public authorities about having a proper celebration commemorating the event. . . .

"I presented a resolution to Congress, made a speech on the floor of the House on Jan. 14, 1897, and the ship was repaired, came to the Charlestown Navy Yard and a fine celebration, at my suggestion, by the city and State authorities, was held. . . .It is my belief that if this work were not done there would be no *Constitution* today."

Constitution more often came closer to destruction in the hands of her own people than through enemy action. It soon became apparent the repairs made at Portsmouth were not sufficient, and by 1905 she was in such a sad state of disrepair it was proposed that she be taken out to sea and used as a target for the fleet.

But the public rebelled over such a fate for the gallant frigate and Congress appropriated $100,000 in 1906 for additional repairs. Thereafter she remained twenty years at her pier in the role of a museum piece, during which time she again almost hopelessly decayed.

Symbol of Sea Power

There was little official enthusiasm for financing reconstruction work needed by *Constitution* in the Twenties. In 1925, Congress enacted a bill authorizing reconstruction but it provided no funds. The bill stated:

"The Secretary of the Navy is. . .authorized to accept and use any donations or contributions which may be offered for the aforesaid purpose."

A nationwide campaign brought contributions of both material and cash. Children sent a deluge of small coins. But what was received fell somewhat short of what was required. The Navy Yard estimate was $650,654; much more was spent before the work was completed. Reconstruction, the most extensive until that date, slowed down or speeded up according to availability of cash and material. After it became apparent contributions would not be sufficient, Congress appropriated funds to complete the work.

On June 16, 1927, *Constitution* returned to Constitution Dry Dock, which she had christened ninety-four years earlier.

RESCUED AGAIN—*Another urgently needed reconstruction was undertaken at the Boston Navy Yard in the 1920's. This extensive rebuilding cost more than $921,000, the bulk of which was raised by contributions of small coins by school children, public subscription, and the sale of souvenirs. Congress was called upon to furnish only $271,000 to complete the work. When placed in drydock in 1927, left, extensive shoring was necessary to sup-port the fragile hull. Decayed timber was removed and replaced with sound material. The interior of the hull also was given extensive support. Skilled wooden-ship builders were recruited wherever those members of a vanishing craft could be found, and much of the country was called upon to furnish necessary material, some of it also scarce. The stern view below is of the old warship four years later after much of the task had been completed.*

The old frigate had become so structurally weak it was feared she might literally fall apart when no longer supported by water. Wooden ships usually are hauled out at frequent intervals for cleaning, painting, and repairs below the waterline, but *Constitution* had not received this attention in many years. Even in 1907 she was considered too fragile for drydocking. But Lieutenant John Lord, the Navy's last wooden-shipbuilder, so effectively supported the ancient hull within and without that there was no mishap.

Then came a quest for material, some of which became difficult to find after the passing of the wooden ship era. For masts, Douglas fir timbers, one 109 feet long, were brought on flatcars from the Pacific Northwest. *Constitution's* original masts were of pine found in Maine, but trees of the size needed had long since been cut down. One critical item, live oak, was located in Commodore's Pond, Pensacola, Florida,

where it had been stored since the 1850's, unused because iron ships supplanted wood.

Lieutenant Lord returned to Bath, Maine, where his family had been shipbuilders for generations, to look for something equally critical—shipwrights skilled in the ancient trade. He recruited some eighty of them and he also found and borrowed the long-unused tools of the craft.

When *Constitution* was floated out of the drydock March 16, 1930, she was as sound as the day of her 1797 launching. Repairs had cost several times her original construction cost.

Constitution left Boston under tow on July 2, 1931, after half a century of inactivity, on one of the longest voyages of her career.

Her new duty, under Commander Louis J. Gulliver, was a tour which took her to ninety ports and brought 4,614,792 visitors aboard. Although in her 134th year, she looked as though she just left her launching ways.

ANCHORS AWEIGH—*Old Ironsides' sailors and marines, backs bending to the task, work capstan bars to bring the frigate's anchor aboard during a cruise which took her to ninety of the nation's ports. At right, in keeping with tradition, the crew mans her yards while getting under way. Millions of visitors who never before had an opportunity to see the famous warship came aboard at ports of call along the East, Gulf, and West Coasts. She left Boston in July 1931 and returned three years later.*

(Editors' note: The author wrote this account of **Constitution's** departure from Boston in 1931 for the Associated Press. It was printed in newspapers throughout the country.)

AVAST, BELAY!

Old Ironsides Sails

By Tom Horgan

Boston, July 2 (AP) — What ship is this? U. S. Frigate **Constitution**, Sir.

Where away? Out of Boston on the afternoon tide, Sir, bound up the coast for Portsmouth, New Hampshire. Due there in the morning.

Stranger in these waters, aye, but stranger in any waters for many a year. Tied up in Boston Navy Yard since 1897, when she came home for her hundredth birthday. Came then under tow, as she is now, from Portsmouth, after some rebuilding in the Navy Yard there.

You ask why she does not cast off the tug **Grebe's** line and break out her own white canvas? Why, bless you Sir, scarce enough men has she aboard to work her weather braces.

Of a truth, she could stand a breeze of wind, as she has often enough in the past. Time was when her scuppers, now riding so high, were rolled down to the chortling sea, but she would not mind that.

Captain Isaac Hull had a crew of 456 when he whipped the **Guerriere**, back in 1812. Now she carries but 85, and a scant 60 of those know aught of sail. She lost seven men in that engagement, and **Guerriere** 15. Not many as reckoned nowadays with rapid-fire and long-range guns, but it was a

merry go. . . .

Aye, her sides are as stout again, and her timbers and spars as well. Lieutenant John A. Lord has seen to that. Lieutenant Lord, with 34 years' service, is the last of the Navy's wooden-ship constructors, and the shade of Joshua Humphreys who designed her, could find no fault with John Lord's work. From stem to stern no unsound bit of timber is in her hull. . . .

Fast? Aye, that she was, and must still be, fast as sailing ships go. And that more than once kept her from destruction when beset by overpowering numbers. . . . Under a press of canvas she logged better than 13 knots, better speed than she's making now under tow. . . .

WELCOME TO NEW YORK—*Fire-boats send plumes of water skyward, offering the city's traditional salute to a sea-borne visitor, as* Constitution *enters New York Harbor. She was met by a marine procession of more than a hundred vessels as whistles shrieked and guns boomed.*

ONE HAND FOR THE SHIP—*The windjammer sailor's rule of "one hand for the ship, one hand for yourself" was often ignored. Above, some of the crew are aloft in a sail-handling exercise. Spread out along a yard, they are furling one of the big square sails—and using both hands for the task. Although* Constitution *carried a full suit of sail during her tour, she was towed throughout the entire trip.* Constitution *has not moved under sail since the nineteenth century.*

93

More than twenty-two thousand sea miles were traveled in three years. Commander Gulliver called it "...the longest and most hazardous towing cruise in history"; it was not marred by a single accident. The towing was by *USS Grebe*, a minesweeper, which had seen service in the North Sea during World War I. The northernmost call on the Atlantic was Bar Harbor, Maine, and on the Pacific, Bellingham, Washington. Balboa, in the Canal Zone, was the southernmost.

Almost two million visitors boarded Old Ironsides in California, the greatest number from any one state. The greatest number of visitors in a single day was 36,400, at San Pedro Harbor, Los Angeles.

Constitution made Portsmouth, New Hampshire, her first port of call, and the enthusiastic reception she received was repeated throughout her entire cruise. Some thirty thousand persons came aboard in five days at Portsmouth, a town that was no stranger to Old Ironsides, for she had been repaired there in 1871 and had reported there again in 1881 as a receiving ship.

Coming down the coast, *Constitution* again called at Marblehead, Massachusetts, the little harbor that had once proved her salvation, in 1814, when it sheltered the ship from two pursuing British frigates.

Old Ironsides made many New England calls and was received with particular enthusiasm at the ancient fishing port of Gloucester, the old whaling capital of New Bedford, and Newport, Rhode Island, a town steeped in naval tradition.

Constitution was met at New York on August 29 by a nautical parade a half mile long of more than a hundred vessels. Military planes formed another procession in the air. Gun salutes were fired ashore and afloat and whistles and sirens added to the din. Uncounted thousands lined waterfront piers and other vantage points as she proceeded to a Hudson River pier. During a two-week stay, more than a hundred thousand visitors came aboard—a figure exceeded later at Philadelphia (154,809), New Orleans (193,881), and San Pedro (478,029).

The warmth of the old frigate's welcome in the South was, in part, because the region had furnished much of her original timber and material used for repairs and rebuildings. She called at Brunswick, Georgia, passing close to St. Simons Island, from which much of the live oak used in construction was obtained.

94

AT THE GOLDEN GATE—*Old Ironsides arrived in San Francisco Bay on March 24, 1933. The Golden Gate Bridge had not yet been built, but construction had begun. Completed in 1937, the world-famous bridge spanned the place where* Constitution *is pictured. The sturdy little minesweeper* Grebe, *which towed the frigate throughout the tour, is at the extreme right.*

At Port St. Joe, Florida, then a community of 851, a total of 7,479 visitors came aboard. An elderly visitor from St. Petersburg reported aboard to Commander Gulliver: "Charles Nowak, Sir. Gun captain, gun number eleven."

Nowak had served aboard nine months in 1882. The 76-year-old veteran gave his old ship a close inspection and had to be persuaded *not* to climb the rigging.

After calls at Gulf ports, *Constitution* shaped a course for the Panama Canal, enroute to the Pacific. She arrived at Cristobal, on the Atlantic, December 23, 1932, where almost every resident must have come aboard. Then she was cautiously towed through the "Big Ditch." She continued her triumphal tour along the West Coast, visiting almost every anchorage with sufficient water to accommodate her deep draft.

By now, the receptions had developed something of a pattern. An official welcoming delegation promptly came aboard. This was followed by representatives of various patriotic, veterans', civic, and service organizations, many with offers of cooperation and entertainment ashore for the ship's company. The ship everywhere proved a prime attraction for children.

Many residents of the Northwest felt they had a proprietary interest in the old warship. Lumbermen of the area had donated five carloads of Douglas fir for the most recent rebuilding, and the railroads had transported the timber to Boston without charge.

After reversing her course at Bellingham, Washington, *Constitution* headed back to New England, calling at some ports she had missed on the outward bound voyage. She returned to her berth at the Boston Navy Yard on May 7, 1934, after a three-year absence to resume her station as one of the nation's historic shrines. Hundreds of thousands of visitors come aboard annually, many of them school children, who are particularly attentive to Navy guides. Since 1940 she has served as flagship for Commandants of the First Naval District.

In the words of an official United States Navy history: ". . . *Constitution* remains in commission today, the oldest ship on the Navy List, [a] proud and worthy representative of the Navy's great days of fighting sail, and [a] symbol of the courage and patriotic service of generations of Americans at sea where much of the Nation's destiny will always lie."

OLD IRONSIDES

Part II

A Contemporary View

WELCOME ABOARD—*No foe has ever trod* Constitution's *deck except as a prisoner of war, but hundreds of thousands of friends come aboard each year as eager visitors. Launched in 1797, she is the oldest warship in any navy still afloat. The role she played under sail in shaping the nation's destiny guarantees her place in history.*

A WARRIOR AT REST—Constitu-
tion, *an enduring symbol of the nation's
sea power, has become one of the country's most important historic shrines.
Hundreds of thousands of visitors from
all the states and many foreign countries tread her decks each year. The
imaginative may hear the roar of gunfire and sniff burned powder, reliving
the days of Old Ironsides' prime when
she wrote some of the nation's most
important pages of sea-faring history.*

A GLIMPSE OF THE PAST—*These
youthful sailors are from the modern
Navy, but they are clad in uniforms of
the style of Constitution's years of glory.
These nine, members of the U. S. Navy
Band from Washington, D.C., took
part in one of the many special events
conducted aboard Old Ironsides—
Easter Sunday sunrise services. Note
the decorative billet head beneath the
bowsprit, a position which was some-
times occupied by a figurehead during
Constitution's sailing career.*

A SHIP'S BOATS—*In the days of sail, a ship carried numerous small boats which performed many tasks. They were, of course, pulling boats — propelled with oars. Constitution customarily carried about eight such craft. The captain's 28-foot gig was carried in davits over the stern. To conserve space, three boats, the largest a 36-foot pinnace, were nested, one inside the other, on the spar deck hatch. At left, one of* Constitution's *boats swings in davits for ease in launching. Below are two boats carried on the spar deck, with the ship's bell mounted in the gallows between them. At right, another view of the boat carried in davits over the starboard side. The small boats assisted in docking the ship by carrying out lines to the pier; they transported supplies and messages between ship and shore and, of course, had the pleasant duty of carrying liberty parties ashore.*

DECK VIEW—*Here, right, is Constitution's spar deck. On either side are carronades, their blunt muzzles protruding through gunports in the high bulwarks. The bulwarks furnished gun-crews some protection, particularly from lighter missiles such as grape shot and musket balls. In the foreground is an elaborate skylight which serves the dual purpose of illuminating and ventilating the captain's quarters on the gun deck below. In the center, partly concealed by the mizzenmast, is Constitution's wheel. Actually, there are two wheels fitted to the same gear, permitting several men to assist in keeping the ship on course in bad weather.*

A SHIP'S SECURITY—Constitution *carried six ponderous anchors. They included two bowers weighing 5,304 pounds each, commonly used in routine anchoring, and a 5,443-pound sheet anchor — a type considered so efficient its name became a synonym for security. The others were a 1,100-pound stream anchor and two kedge anchors, one 700 pounds and one 403 pounds. The weight of the anchors and necessary gear explains why as many as 180 men might be assigned to the anchor detail. At left is* Constitution's *port cathead, a stout timber to which tackle was attached to haul an anchor to deck level to stow it; this was a chore known as "catting the anchor." At upper right is one of her anchors after being brought aboard and firmly secured to the deck. At lower right, a modern sailor (in early Navy uniform) inspects a section of anchor cable such as* Constitution *used in wartime. It is twenty-two inches in circumference.*

DECK SCENE—*The platform below was a nerve center in the operation of a fighting ship such as* Constitution. *There stood the sailing master, a man uncommonly knowledgeable in the handling of the many complexities of the rigging which controlled the set of the sails. From here he trumpeted orders to the crew, some high aloft in the tops. Often, in battle, he had no time to weigh his decisions, yet any mistake could spell disaster. Usually this important post was occupied by a warrant officer. At right, a sailor stands beneath the mizzenboom, from which was set one of the few sails* Constitution *carried which was not cut square. At far right is a section of the pinrail around the mizzenmast, where running rigging was secured to belaying pins. The light line is a flag halyard.*

106

IRON DOGS—*The two photos at left are of carronades on the spar deck. Note the priming pan beneath the sailor's fingers in the top picture. After the weapon was charged with powder and shot, gunpowder was put into this pan, using a powder horn, right. Below, a sailor demonstrates how the guns were fired. A burning "slow match" was touched to the powder in the priming pan, exploding the main charge within the gun. The close-up on the opposite page clearly shows the quoin, or wedge, used to adjust the gun's elevation. The heavy piece of cordage checked the carronade's recoil when fired.*

FIREPOWER—*Above left, five long guns protrude through closed ports from* Constitution's *gun deck, where her heaviest armament is mounted. Over them are several stubby carronades peering from spar deck gunports. Although* Constitution *was designed as a 44-gun frigate, it is doubtful if she ever carried precisely that number. She mounted fifty-five guns when she destroyed* Guerriere *and about the same when she defeated* Java. *Included were thirty 24-pounders on the gun deck and twenty-two 32-pound carronades on the spar, or upper deck, plus two long 24-pounders and a long 18-pounder on the spar deck. At left is the gun deck.*

WEIGHT OF METAL—*The long guns have a bore of a little under six inches and are more than nine feet long. They used about six pounds of powder as a charge for an estimated range of twelve hundred yards. The carronades have a bore of a little more than six inches and were charged with about two and a half pounds of powder. They are much shorter — a bit over four feet — and had a correspondingly shorter range, slightly under four hundred yards. At close quarters, carronades were most destructive, their heavier shot having a crushing rather than penetrating effect. Being much lighter they were more easily handled and could be fired faster than the long guns. A carronade weighs 2,175 pounds compared with a long gun's 5,730. Above is a close-up of one of the long 24-pounders.*

GUNPOWDER—*Magazines were located deep in* Constitution's *hold, with explosives stored in wooden casks (below). Young lads rushed powder charges to the guns in leather buckets such as the one at right. The powder monkeys fully realized the hazards of their task and cautiously shielded the buckets from stray sparks with their jackets as they raced up ladders from the magazines to the guns. A powder monkey was included in each gun crew and in action he was a very busy youngster.*

IRON—*Aboard* Constitution *today is an extensive collection of relics of the days of the sailing ship navy. Here are racks of cutlasses, cannon balls, and a variety of special purpose missiles. Bar shot, somewhat resembling a long-stemmed wine glass, was fashioned from two halves of a cannon ball connected by an iron rod and was especially effective against masts and rigging. Projectiles also included cannister and chain shot. Cannister shot consisted of a large number of iron balls in a container which burst after leaving a gun's muzzle. The contents scattered in much the same way as a shotgun charge. Chain shot was similar to bar, except that chain was used in place of a connecting rod. It also was used to destroy rigging.*

SMALL ARMS—Constitution's *most useful weapons were her guns, but she also carried a variety of small arms. These included cutlasses, boarding pikes, flintlock pistols, and muskets, above and right. Except for the long-barreled muskets, small arms were of little value to the frigate. Her commanders were little influenced by the British doctrine of naval warfare, which was to quickly close with and board the enemy. Instead, they preferred to stand outside carronade range and soften up the foe with deliberately aimed long guns. Then* Constitution *came into point-blank carronade range and pounded her enemy into submission without boarding.*

THE COMMODORE'S CABIN—
Here, below, the senior officer aboard transacted his business and received many important callers. The treaty of peace with Tripoli was signed here in June of 1805. The commander shared these quarters with four long guns, two 24-pounders on either side of the compartment. During Constitution's *active service, illumination was furnished by oil lamps similar to the one at right. This brass lamp swings in gimbals and is designed to remain upright despite the rolling and pitching of the ship.*

THE CAPTAIN'S QUARTERS—
Living accommodations for the officers who directed Constitution *are aft on the gun deck. Off this section of the captain's cabin, left, is his sleeping compartment, right. The wooden grillwork furnished light and ventilation. Similar appointments beyond the opposite end of the cabin were designated for a commodore's use in the event the frigate had both captain and commodore aboard while serving as a flagship. Below left, a sailor peers over the stern from the captain's cabin.*

DECORATIONS—*During periods when* Constitution *did not carry a figurehead, her bow usually was graced by a billet or fiddlehead. The billet head below was installed in 1876 during restoration of the ship at the Philadelphia Navy Yard, succeeding a figurehead of Andrew Jackson. The billet head, at left, took its place in 1906, at the Boston Navy Yard, serving until extensive reconstruction began in the 1920's. These two wood carvings remain aboard on exhibit.*

MANNING THE CAPSTAN—*At left, sailors of a later generation demonstrate how* Constitution *got her anchor up when ready to sail in the days when ships relied entirely on manpower. Twelve capstan bars—long poles— were inserted in pigeonholes over the wasp-waisted drum. Turns of the huge anchor cable were taken around the drum and it was inched in, as a large detail of the ship's company marched around the capstan, bringing the ponderous two-and-one-half ton mud hook up from the bottom. The frigate has two capstans, this one on the gun deck, another above on the spar deck, both mounted on the same vertical shaft. The gun deck capstan was used chiefly to handle anchors; that on the spar deck for a variety of heavy work, including hauling on running rigging and docking lines.*

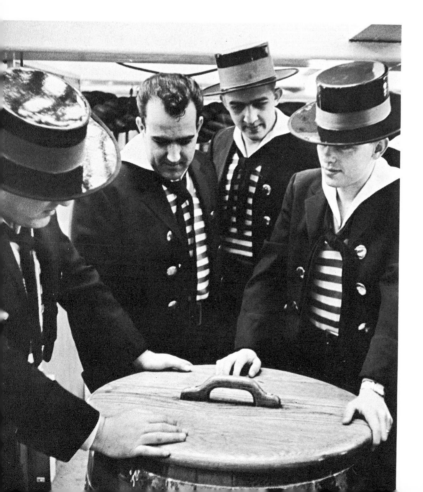

WET STORES—*Without refrigeration, a monotonous diet was unavoidable. Most provisions were salted or dried. "Old salts" liked to claim they had seen food come aboard labeled "Unfit for human consumption, but good enough for sailors." Whether fact or fancy, the sailors nicknamed the barrels of salted meat "harness casks," saying the toughness of the contents was due to the suppliers' having neglected to remove the leather harnesses of the "horses" they had packed. Beside the grog-tub, above, is a scuttlebutt, from which fresh water was rationed. The ship could carry 48,600 gallons. She also sailed with about 4,500 gallons of spirits, dispensing about twenty-five gallons daily from the grog-tub.*

THE MENU

Constitution's crew did not fare badly considering the times. Here are the daily rations prescribed for each man:

Sunday: 1¼ lbs. beef, 14 oz. bread, ½ lb. flour, ¼ lb. suet, ½ pt. spirits.

Monday: 1 lb. pork, 14 oz. bread, ½ pt. peas, ½ pt. spirits.

Tuesday: 1 lb. beef, 14 oz. bread, 2 oz. cheese, ½ pt. spirits.

Wednesday: 1 lb. pork, 14 oz. bread, ½ pt. rice, ½ pt. spirits.

Thursday: 1¼ lb. beef, 14 oz. bread, ½ lb. flour, ¼ lb. suet, ½ pt. spirits.

Friday: 14 oz. bread, ½ pt. rice, 4 oz. cheese, 2 oz. butter, ½ pt. molasses, ½ pt. spirits.

Saturday: 1 lb. pork, 14 oz. bread, ½ pt. peas, ½ pt. vinegar, ½ pt. spirits.

THE COOKS' DOMAIN—*Food was prepared on a big wood-burning stove in the galley located on the gun deck. The cooks leaned heavily toward soups and stews to satisfy more than four hundred robust appetites. An important part of a cook's task was to first soak some of the salt out of preserved meat. Large quantities of cord wood were carried in the hold to stoke the galley stove. The rack around the hatch in front of the stove holds a supply of 24-pound solid shot. The anchor chain in the picture is modern — cordage was used during* Constitution's *active years.*

NO FRILLS HERE—*With a crew of well over four hundred, quarters were extremely limited. The enlisted man's bed was a swaying hammock, here lashed beneath the overhead for stowage. Each man was assigned a sleeping space roughly eight feet long and two feet wide on the poorly ventilated berth deck. Some fresh air was funneled to these quarters from wind scoops rigged on the spar deck. Sleeping on the gun deck was permitted by some commanders. There, weather permitting, gun ports could be opened to admit fresh air.*

122

WARDROOM AND ORLOP DECK—
Junior officers congregated in the ward-room, above, located on the berth deck. This was where they dined, the center of their leisure hours at sea, and where they received visitors in port. Their small staterooms adjoin the ward-room behind wooden grillwork and barely have room for a small bed and some personal effects. Below the berth deck is the orlop deck, lowest in the ship and used chiefly for storage. The group at right cannot even stand erect in one of the small storerooms on the orlop deck. Fire has always been a major hazard to wooden ships, and Constitution *is now protected by a sprinkler system. A sailor here has his hand on one of the sprinkler pipes.*

ANNUAL "CRUISE"—*Her guns no longer thunder, but Old Ironsides rests securely in a niche of history she fashioned for herself. Cherished by a nation she helped establish as a first-rate power, every measure is taken to preserve the ancient warship. The weather has become her most dangerous foe. For that reason, her position at her pier is reversed annually. This is intended to equalize her exposure over the years to the rigors of the elements and to avoid unbalanced warping by sun and storm. Thus, she alternately presents her port or starboard side to the rising sun. Her annual turn-around, when tugs take her out of her berth for a brief "cruise," has become a picturesque ceremony.*

Acknowledgments

So much has been written and recited about the career of the nation's most famous warship — *USS Constitution* — that inevitably conflicts and disagreements have intruded. This volume is an effort to present a concise and reliable version. Much of Old Ironsides' story has filtered down the years with scant documentation and the most challenging phase of this task has been to separate fact from fable, or even fiction. In striving for this objective, unstinted assistance and encouragement from many sources is gratefully acknowledged. We particularly wish to thank:

Rear Admiral Ernest M. Eller, Director of Naval History and Curator for the Navy Department, for reviewing the manuscript.

Rear Admiral Joseph H. Wellings, Commandant of the First Naval District at the inception of this volume, who furnished valued advice and support.

Commander George M. Hall, former Public Information Officer of the First Naval District, for his able assistance and encouragement, from the origin of the idea through to the completion of the book.

Lieutenant Victor B. Stevens, *Constitution's* Commanding Officer while the book was in preparation, for his complete cooperation and for supplying original source material available only aboard the ship.

Commander John D. McKinnon, Commanding Officer of *Constitution* when the final photographs and material were being developed, for his aid and suggestions made while he was preparing the ship for a major overhaul.

Mr. Fred Cummings of the Boston Naval Shipyard; Lieutenant Commander David M. Cooney and Lieutenant Francis X. Steele of the Navy's Office of Information; Lieutenant Beverly W. Frost, of the First Naval District's Public Information Office; Mr. Henry A. Vadnais, Jr. of the Office of Naval History; Lieutenant Commander J. William Stierman, USN; and Mr. Milton Kaplan, of the Library of Congress

T. P. Horgan

T. Thomte

Index

Illustration Credits

All the photographs that appear in the illustrated introduction are the work of Commander George M. Hall USN(Ret.). His long-time knowledge of the ship, coupled with his artistic skill, made it possible for us to capture some of the feeling of men who have known Old Ironsides.

The majority of the photographs appearing in Part II of this volume were the work of one man Frank Blaha Denman, of Boston. The publisher is indebted to Mr. Denman for his talented assistance, cooperation, and artistic appreciation of the subject.

George M. Hall: 10-34.

Frank B. Denman: 37, 100, 102-109, 112, 113, 114 bottom, 115 top, 116 bottom, 117-120, 122, 123 bottom, 126.

John Hancock Mutual Life Insurance Company: Back Jacket. Library of Congress: 49, 54-55, 62 top, 78, 80, 81, 83, 85-87, 90-92. U. S. Navy — Mariners Museum, Newport News, Virginia: 52. National Archives: 40, 46-47. New England Mutual Life Insurance Company: 43. The New York Historical Society, New York City: 73. U. S. Marine Corps: 60, 61. U. S. Navy: 39, 41, 44, 45, 50, 56-57, 59, 62 bottom, 64-65, 67-71, 74-75, 77, 84, 88, 89, 93-96, 98-99, 101, 110, 111, 114 top, 115 bottom, 116 top, 121, 123 top, 124, 125.